MISSING IN ACTION

MISSING IN ACTION

MAY-SEPTEMBER 1944

PEGGY RYLE

WH Allen · London
A Howard & Wyndham Company
1979

Printed and bound in Great Britain by
Butler & Tanner Ltd, Frome and London
for the Publishers
W. H. Allen & Co. Ltd, 44 Hill Street
London W1X 8LB

ISBN 0 491 02168 2

For Georgie

INTRODUCTION

Many people keep a diary at some time in their lives, but very rarely are they read by other people – it's the sort of personal thing that you keep tucked away with old photographs, letters and other personal bits and pieces. Sometimes they get turned out, glanced at, giggled over and even the odd tear may be shed for times gone by – but they don't often get published for everybody to read.

It was on one of these 'turning out' days that I came across this diary and asked my mother about it. She gave it to me to read. At first I didn't want to – how could I read her private diary. But she insisted as she felt that it was a few months in her life that at the time, although I was very closely involved, I had been too young really to understand. So I found myself reading a very personal and private 'conversation' between my mother and my stepfather (a one-sided conversation I know) but I really did get this overwhelming feeling that she was talking to him.

There have been many books written about the heroes of the Second World War, but not so many about the women they left behind them, waiting, not knowing when or if their men would return. In my opinion those women were equally heroic but are perhaps too often forgotten. I would like their grandchildren and great-grandchildren to know what war was really like for them and I believe that this diary can give them a small insight into this. My mother's entries in the diary take place over a very short period of time, but when you are waiting for someone you love, a few months must seem like a lifetime.

In 1944, even if the world was tumbling around you, you did not show your feelings to anyone, least of all the children. Everybody else had worries of their own and if you had a problem you just had to try and sort it out on your own. Through this diary, my mother could let her husband know her true feelings and sufferings and, by putting these feelings down on paper, she could relieve some of the tension and emotion that she felt. Sitting by herself at night she could go through the day to day happenings with him, tell him about things that she had to cope with in his absence, and above all pray for his quick return.

My parents had divorced at the beginning of the war and Georgie was now my stepfather. He was six months older than my mother, although the records at the Air Ministry would show him as being two years younger than her – he altered his papers so that he could go on active service and not just have a desk job in the RAF. So really 9th May 1944 was his thirty-eighth birthday. Physically, I don't think Georgie could be called handsome – nice looking perhaps. He was about six foot tall and considerably overweight at the beginning of the war. To become a rear gunner he had to lose nearly two stone to enable him to get into the rear turret –

the entrance to which was exceedingly small! I think my mother was attracted to him by his wonderful sense of humour and enjoyment in living – he was always smiling and I don't ever remember him being cross or bad tempered with anyone. Having married my mother he found himself with a ready-made family – my sister and myself – and when people referred to us as his daughters, he never told them that we were really his step-children. He was very proud of us and when somebody would comment on how much I looked like him he would give me a quick wink which meant 'don't tell' – it became our own private joke. We were a very close little family.

In the early part of 1943, when he had been flying on operations for longer than was usual, Georgie was posted to the Air Ministry in London which he disliked intensely. We moved into a flat in Queen's Gate, but we all missed the country and London was very boring for children during the war – we were used to swimming, riding, and an active outdoor life. So, every morning on the way to the Air Ministry Georgie used to take us to the Serpentine so that we could all have an hour or so swimming and then he would go on to work and in the evenings he would always find time before we went to bed to play and joke with us girls. Georgie was our great playmate: it would always be he, who would come into the stream and help us build dams, he who would find an old tin hip bath that we could sail down the stream in, and he who bought me my first pony.

Mother, in her mid-thirties, was still a very beautiful woman. She had a wonderful complexion and greeny hazel eyes. There was nothing sophisticated about her, she was always absolutely natural, with an exceptional ability to make friends: in fact they both had an unusual number of true and close friends. They were both people with a great sense of humour and a zest for life, in particular their life together. Whenever they were together it was all laughter and sunshine even if bombs were falling and planes crashing.

When I see films now about the RAF in the last war it all comes rushing back to me and reading this diary makes it even more vivid – the noise of the guns and bombs, but above all the doodlebugs – the strange whine of their engines and then those terrible seconds of silence when you waited for the explosion with your heart in your mouth. Nowadays I can barely tell the difference between a jumbo jet and a concorde, but in those days I think most children (and I certainly could) were able to tell the difference between a Spitfire and a Messerschmitt by sight. Also, just by the noise of the engines you knew if it was an enemy plane or not flying overhead at night.

The skies would be alive with different noises as my mother sat alone each night pouring out her heart to her husband. But it had not been all guns and bombs; there had been many weeks of happiness spent in houses dotted around England. Wherever Georgie was stationed, mother would rent a furnished house nearby and then my sister and myself would go there for our school holidays. These rented houses near the RAF stations would always be full of people – anyone, from the Squadron who had weekend leave (those precious 48 hours) but whose home was too far to get to, would always be welcome at the Ryle's house. My sister and I would get to know many of the pilots, gunners and navigators most of whom were much younger than Mummy and Georgie. Some of them would become very special friends. Perhaps they had younger sisters at home and were used to playing kids' games and were happy keeping us amused. But like many good things, these special friendships would not last forever, they wouldn't be around any more – they would be reported missing. Mother never told us the true facts, she would say they had been posted to another station. It was only when the war was over and we were both old enough to understand more about death that Mother explained that they had been killed.

Reading the diary, I was startled by the difference in our society and our way of life today compared with thirty-five years ago. It is really a short time, but what a very different attitude to everything we all had then – I am sure some people today would think of it as practically Victorian. A good example is the whole matter of divorce. In the early 1940s it was a subject that you kept very quiet about, it was hidden under the carpet, something not to be discussed. I am sure that when my father divorced my mother she had no idea how it would affect her future, particularly the fact that *he* had divorced her. Obviously, while she was with Georgie he protected her from any comments, but during the months that she was writing this diary and he was away from her for the first time since their marriage, she soon found out. She was a woman who had admitted committing adultery and whose husband had divorced her (although he was equally guilty, but the gossips didn't know that) and she was therefore more or less branded as a scarlet woman.

My parents' marriage was not happy. I can't help feeling that in the same situation nowadays nobody would think twice about divorcing – and from reading this diary, I now understand why they took so much trouble over telling us children of their divorce and pending remarriages. We all went away for the weekend together to stay at a hotel in Worthing, and there, after a few happy hours altogether, Mummy and Daddy called us to their room and told us to sit down – all very solemn – as they had something to tell us that was very important. And so the news was broken. My sister being that much older than me and more able to understand the meaning of it all, was thoroughly upset. I wasn't. I remember feeling I would be 'one up' on my friends by having two sets of parents! If I had been asked to adopt a father I am sure I would have chosen Georgie – he had spent many weekends with us in the country and we really loved him, he was always so natural with us children. So now I had another father and as far as I was concerned they were both as good as each other. My future stepmother I had not yet met, but being a girl I was really only interested in fathers.

Stepmothers were people that I had read about in books and seen in pantomimes like 'Cinderella' – if I was going to end up a Cinderella I would also end up with the prince, so that was no problem. Anyhow, we children were going to live with Mummy and Georgie which didn't sound like a life of washing floors and dishes to me!

I think the effect of her divorce on other people and their sometimes cruel comments were softened to some extent for my mother by the fact that she remained very close friends with her ex-parents-in-law and her two ex-sisters-in-law, all of whom stood by her and went on being 'family' to her. Perhaps in those days they were even putting their own reputations in jeopardy by remaining such close friends with Mummy.

When I had finished reading the diary, I remember putting it down and wishing that I had been a few years older at the time so that I could have been of some help, somewhere, somehow. In all those awful months I only saw my mother cry once and that was entirely my fault. It must have been about two days after Georgie was reported missing and it was a very warm day. Mummy was sitting in the garden with some friends who had come round to keep her company, when she asked me to go upstairs and fetch her a sun hat. She was sitting close to the house, right below her bedroom window. Having found the hat, I looked out of the window and there she was. To get it to her quickly I leant out of the window and with very careful aim, dropped it right on to her head. She must have been close to breaking point because she immediately burst into tears from fright and shock. It was something that she would never normally have done and I hardly ever saw her do it again, not even during or after the six months that followed – six months of worry, misery and loneliness.

THE MAIN CHARACTERS

Peggy Ryle
Born 4th November 1906. Married to Donald Shuter. Two daughters by this marriage, Day born 6th May 1929 and Sally, born 9th September 1932. Educated at Upper Chine in Shanklin, Isle of Wight, where she was Head Girl. No profession apart from housewife and mother. Divorced Don Shuter and married George Ryle in 1942.

George Ryle
Born 9th May 1906 (as far as the RAF was concerned he changed this date to 1908). Educated Manchester Grammar School. Commissioned in May 1940, took part in the first raid over Berlin and after about twenty-five operations over Germany went to Malta. Posted to Greece where he was mentioned in dispatches in September 1941 for an operation on Rhodes from which he returned after bombing at 1,000 feet and machine gunning aircraft on the ground at 200 feet with his machine holed in sixteen places and both engines punctured. He received the Distinguished Flying Cross after operations in January 1944 for high skill, fortitude and devotion to duty. Married Peggy after her divorce (stepfather to Day and Sally).

Sally Shuter (Sal)
Younger daughter of Peggy Ryle and Don Shuter.
Educated at her mother's old school Upper Chine to
start with and then Byculla.

Arthur Granville Martin
Father of Peggy Ryle, an Antique dealer living in Surbiton, married to Jean, his third wife.

Judy Lockhart
Married to Wing Commander Guy Lockhart, pilot of
the plane on which George Ryle was Rear Gunner,
reported missing over Friedrichshafen.

Judy Ryle
George Ryle's half sister.

Kate Ryle
George Ryle's mother.

Isadore
Worked for the company that George Ryle worked for
in peacetime – Green Hearn and Co. Ltd.

Charles Shuter (the old man)
Peggy Ryle's ex-father-in-law. Owner of Shuter and
Gibbons (S & G's), a dress manufacturing company.

Marjorie Hughes
A Buyer for one of the leading West End stores.

Muriel
Peggy Ryle's ex-sister-in-law married to Henry Butter-field, working for her father at Shuter and Gibbons.

Stodge
Muriel's sister (ex-sister-in-law of Peggy) also working in the Rag Trade.

Jo
Sally's spaniel puppy.

Ray Ridley
George Ryle's closest friend, also 'missing', had been stationed at Oakington with George.

Bodger
The Ryle's Bank Manager.

Jean Granville Martin
Peggy Ryle's step-step mother.

Day Shuter
Elder daughter of Peggy Ryle and Don Shuter. Origin-ally educated at Upper Chine with Sally but now the two girls are at separate schools.

Bargie
Friend of the Granville Martin family who had had close relationship with Peggy Ryle's uncle who had recently died ... Uncle Jack.

Chris's Wife
Chris was a crew member of the same plane as George, which is missing.

Toppy Bryant
A close friend of the Shuters and the Ryles, married to Peter, living in a village called Abbotts Ann near the village where the Shuters had a cottage, which was sold after Don and Peggy divorced – freelance Harvesting Contractors.

Barbara Ryle
George Ryle's sister.

Shuter Fashions
Donald Shuter's model gown manufacturing company run by Peggy Ryle when he joined the RAF but taken over by Carol when Peggy married George.

Carol Shuter
Donald Shuter's second wife (stepmother to Day and Sally).

Miss Nagel (Nags)
Headmistress of Byculla school where Sally is now.

Miss Robley Brown (R.B.)
Headmistress of Day's school

Fred and Mabel
Husband and wife who are Landlords of the Black Swan in Monxton (the Duck).

THE MAIN CHARACTERS

Gordon Harker
One of England's best known actors, who had a cottage in Monxton.

Bill Linnit
Theatrical Impressario and Agent who also had a cottage in Monxton.

David and Oakie
Husband and wife who owned a large poultry farm in a village near Monxton.

Deb and Roland (Roley)
Husband and wife. Roland was Gordon Harker's brother and equally well known in the theatre world as a scenic artist – currently camouflaging machine gun posts, etc. also with a cottage in Monxton.

Chris Harker
Gordon's wife and very close friend of Peggy's.

Hugh Granville Martin
Peggy's younger brother, serving in the Army.

The Roberts
Tenants of Peggy and George's flat in Queen's Gate, London.

Little John
Stodge's son, Day and Sally's cousin.

MAY

Your birthday, darling, and I don't know where you are or even if you are alive, although all this week I have had a premonition that you are, and are trying to get to me to feel that you are not dead. Please God I am right.

As I can't give you a birthday present, I thought at least I could keep a diary telling you all I have done since that ghastly morning, Friday 28th April.

That night I slept more deeply than I usually do, but woke up with a start at 2.45 am. From 4 am until 8.25 I walked about the house waiting for you. You had said you were going to be very late so until 7.30 am I did not really start to worry. I still had some comfort from the fact that no one from Oakington had phoned and you had said they would if you were one hour overdue! By 8.25 am however, I could bear it no longer, so I phoned the Mess. The Scots telephonist answered and I asked for you. I waited ages and knew then something had happened. I kept saying to myself, 'This is it. This is it.' Then Dickey came to the phone and I asked where you were. He said, 'Haven't they phoned you, Peg?' – so I knew. He had only just come down and heard himself. I went upstairs and told Sally. Then I went down on my knees and prayed and prayed.

23

During the morning, Dickey came over. He brought me two bottles of gin and two of whisky, but I made up my mind then and there not to drink until we could do so together. I may have an occasional glass of beer, but that will be all, dearest. If *you* can't have it, I don't want it. Group Captain Combes came over in the late morning and was very shy and awkward. I phoned Daddy to ask him to come and spend the night with me so that I could talk things over with him and try and sort myself out. He came and was sweet. But before he arrived, Judy Lockhart and her sister came down from the Mess to see me. The Group Captain had done his damnedest not to give her my address, but she insisted upon having it and now I am thankful, although it seemed rather dreadful at the time. She never stopped laughing and talking, looked more flashy than ever, and simply reeked of a very heavy perfume. Anyway, she did comfort me a little when she told me she was in touch with Guy's former boss, who was in touch with the French underground, and your names might come through quickly that way.

On Saturday 29th April, Daddy went back in the morning and I phoned Mrs Evered and told her she could take over this place, 9 Hill Avenue, from Monday 8th May. I went to see Gray, Son & Cook, and told them I wanted them to release me from the lease.

I forgot to tell you that on Friday morning I phoned Judy, to tell her you were missing, and got her to tell Kate, as I thought it would be less of a shock. I phoned Isadore and asked him to tell Bodger and the boys.

On Saturday evening, the Group Captain, Bob Hunt and the doc. came over and brought chocolates and oranges and did all they could to show their appreciation of the way I was keeping my chin up. I didn't let you down, Georgie. I think you would have been proud of me. The Group Captain told Judy Lockhart I was taking it very well. But none of them can possibly know what an awful agony it is. I have heard people talk of heart-ache and never known what it meant or thought anything about it. But I have a pain round my heart night and day and I feel raw inside.

I have lost a stone and a half in ten days. Nig asked me to stay with her when I got back from Surbiton. I took Sally to Surbiton, and Jo, on that Sunday, saw Sally off on Monday and went into Shuter and Gibbons afterwards to ask old man Shuter's advice about going into Green Hearns and asking for your job. He advised me to wait till the end of the week. It was a bit too soon, he thought. I had lunch with Muriel and they were all extraordinarily nice.

On Tuesday, I lunched with Stodge and asked her if she could have Jo at Pulborough, as Daddy had, bless his heart, taken it for granted I should return to Surbiton with the children and the dog. Stodge arranged that; I don't know what Sal will say as she is devoted to that dog. She was such a good girl and so kind to me during those ghastly days. I also put off going down to see Bodger till this week. I forgot to tell you, I phoned

Hal Lawson on Friday, as he is about the only person I know left at the Air Ministry, and asked him to try and find out anything he could.

On the Saturday night before I took Sally to Surbiton, a most extraordinary thing happened. Sal and I had gone to bed about 10.30 pm when there was a knock on the door and a telegraph man stood there. Sally went down and brought up to me an enormous telegram with red labels and 'Government. Absolute Priority' all over it. It was a pre-paid wire asking if I, Mrs P. D. Ryle, knew the name of the person living at 19/21 Great Portland Street! I presumed you must have put that address when you filled in the people to be told if you were ever missing. So I wired back: '19/21 Great Portland Street business premises. I am S. L. Ryle's second wife, formerly Peggy Shuter, working there. If any news, phone Elm 4203 or wire Ryle, 11 South Bank Lodge, Surbiton.' That seemed to tell them everything they could wish to know.

I returned to Nig's on Tuesday night and stayed with her till Friday morning, spending each day packing up and cleaning up. She lent me two trunks and Daddy, one. The Group Captain was marvellous – he let me have RAF transport. You know both cars were in bits. He had them both overhauled by the transport people. Dickey has put the Ford in Nig's garage and Bob Hunt has bought the Morris for what you originally paid for it. The Group Captain was worried about your gun and I told him Ray's was somewhere about. They found two in Chris's room and I phoned Daddy Ridley and sorted out which was which. I can't remember what you told me about this gun with the chased barrels, but the Group Captain says it is better than Ray's! So it looks as if we have made a gun. I don't think it is your old one, is it?

All that first week, darling, I could not feel anything one way or the other as to whether you were alive or dead, but *everyone* genuinely has the feeling that you are O.K. This week I feel as if you are willing me to know you are trying to get back to me.

On Sunday night Judy Lockhart phoned to say they now have all the names of the planes that came down in Switzerland and that yours was not among them. I was so frightened you might have come down in Lake Constance without your Mae West. But only one crew did that and they swam ashore – Australians and Canadians. I try to keep my mind off all the awful things that may have happened to you, because if I think too much, I shall go off my head.

When I was a little girl, and anything awful had happened, I used to go to sleep and wake up cheerful and then the memory of the awful thing would suddenly flood all over me. With this, I never lose the pain or worry, waking or sleeping – though I don't seem to sleep much. The doctor has given me some sleeping pills (would not let me have the Neurinase you left in the bar!).

Yesterday I thought I would approach Green Hearn. It was rather a toss up whether it was a good time or

27

not because they had had a ghastly case on Friday the details of which I'm not sure about. They were fined £29,160. All directors £4,000 odd, Isadore about £2,000. Bad luck, but looked nasty to the public.

Anyway, I went in and asked for Isadore. He came into the showroom looking as white as a ghost. I think he thought I had had bad news of you. He was very nice and was someone, again, who felt you were all right. I forgot to tell you he phoned me that awful Friday night to ask for more details and say they would offer prayers for you in the Synagogue. Anyhow, he said what a ghastly four days they had had in court and how he wished you had been there to give them a cheery word, so I said that was partly why I had gone in, because I knew at a time like this you would have rallied round, and I must have work to ease my mind – could I help them by doing your job?

In the afternoon, I went to see Lionel. He was grand. Asked me if there was anything he could do and how was I off for money? Did I want any? He told me to leave him my address and Kelsall would send on any money there was, etc. I told him about working and what I had said to Isadore and he said he thought it a good idea, and would speak to Isadore himself.

I also went to Bodger in the afternoon. He was a pet, too. Shoved the balance sheet under my nose with a balance of £1 12s 4d! Said he did not know what happened about pay, so I told him the Group Captain said I will get your marriage allowances and two-sevenths of your pay. We had thought that all your pay would

28

go straight into the bank and I would not be able to draw it out. I had a notice from the Air Ministry today enclosing a form saying your emoluments had stopped and if I wanted an allowance to apply to them and fill in the form, which I have done.

Anyway, to return to Bodger. He suddenly barked at me, 'Got any money?' So I said about £200. 'Got a job?' So I said no, not now and told him I had been to Green Hearns. Not a bad idea, he thought, but as I was a woman, wouldn't be much use to them after the war if you were not coming back. Anyway, before I left he was agreeing with me it was a good thing and I gave him those two bonus certificates of yours for £42 and he gave me the address of the firm's accountants to send your income tax forms to. Told me to pay gas, coal and leave anything else till next month. Anyway I should be all right while the flat is let.

Today my beloved, it's your birthday and I am by myself! Daddy has gone to Brighton, Jean to London, so I can write this. I advertised that blue tweed three-piece in *The Lady* and funnily enough one of the replies came from Surbiton, so I told the woman to come and see it, which she has done and I have just sold it for 12 guineas! Not bad considering you had it made for me about seven years ago and it only cost about 6 guineas then! Bet old Jean is wild her sister turned it down at 8 guineas.

I shall read this afternoon or go to the pictures and go to Muriel and Henry's tonight for grub. I must keep occupied and be with people. Darling, if you have been killed, I don't want to go on living, but I don't believe you have been or I should feel you nearer me, I'm sure. I lie in bed and try and will you, if you are dead, to come and see me and let me see you. One thing I hope, when the time comes for us to die, I go first, I couldn't live through this again. But for now I will try and add to this each day, darling Georgie, so that when you come home, you will know exactly what your Pippy has been doing.

On Day's birthday, I felt so strongly you asked me to wish her a happy one, it will be fun finding out if any of these feelings are true or just imagination when you come back. I have given Daddy your tobacco and an odd bottle of whisky, but he insists they are only lent!

The most wonderful thing happened on Saturday. A certificate came from Don Bennett awarding you the one thing you have always wanted – a *Permanent Path Finder* badge. Also a letter from the Adjutant saying if news comes through that you are a POW I must not tell you under any circumstances. Please God, you will come home to know about it.

10th May

I went to bridge and dinner with Muriel and Henry last night as Jean was out and Daddy in Brighton. A Mrs Peters made up the fourth. It helped me not to think so much.

Today I have been to town. I went to see Marjorie Hughes, as I thought it a good thing to be in with her if I work for Green Hearn. She was charming and full of hope. From there, I went to the flat for the kids' tennis raquets and then to Shuter and Gibbons to pick up Muriel for lunch. Afterwards I went to Wallace Heaton's to have a snap of you and Ray enlarged. Mr Heaton, whom Stodge knows, was out, so will go again on Monday. Then to Stocks to have a new strap on your watch, which I am wearing, and a pin on that *Path Finder* badge you brought home the other night. Such a little while ago, darling, and it seems a lifetime. I think in my innermost heart, I must expect you back or I should never have thought of writing a diary. I have never kept one for more than a few days while I was at school.

I went to see Milly on my way from Kensington to the flat, to see if they had any of that green asparagus we had last year. I thought Daddy would enjoy it. She was delighted to see me and so upset about you. Said she would pray for you, which I thought was sweet of her. Nellie wants me to phone her when I have news. Everyone loves you, darling. Have not yet had a letter from Gray, Son & Cook releasing me from my agreement. Hope there will not be any complications there.

11.30 pm. Just to tell you, darling, how I am longing for you. Did I tell you I wear my little brooch night and day? I feel it may bring you luck. I am keeping this book with all my papers in your despatch case. So I am afraid it will be a bit worn when next you see it. I have been praying so hard, my beloved, that this confidence in your being alive may not be false. Please

God, it is He giving me this belief, and not just wishful thinking.

Oh Georgie, Georgie, where are you?

11th May

10.30 pm. A very quiet day, darling. Did some washing this morning, then went to Food Office to get myself re-registered. Over to the shop and then to some ghastly little café with Daddy and Jean for lunch. I upset them by asking for coffee only. I can't eat now you are away, darling. In the afternoon went to an auction at Kingston. This was held under a glass roof and as it is very sunny today, I nearly fainted. When we returned, I changed into my old, spotted, navy and white dress and, wonders of wonders, while we were playing solo, I felt in the pocket and there was a whole partridge wishbone! Dearest, I feel this is a good omen and am so excited about it. How on earth could it have got into a *summer* frock?

Had a letter from Kelsall today enclosing a cheque for £28 odd, being £50 on commission less PAYE. It was sweet of Lionel. Kelsall says in his letter to call for your money whenever I want any. Jolly good of them, Georgie. There was also a letter from the RAF Benevolent Fund asking if I needed any assistance. The only assistance I want is in finding you. Oh, please God, this wishbone means something good.

Goodnight, my own beloved husband.

12th May   10.30 pm

Oh, what a long week. Georgie darling, it is only two weeks today since you didn't come home to me and it feels like two years. This morning I went to Kingston with Jean. Terribly hot, couldn't eat any lunch, so came home and went to sleep this afternoon. Wish I could go to sleep till good news of you comes through. I think I shall try and die if you are not coming back to me, beloved.

Tonight Bargie phoned for Daddy and me to go to tea on Sunday. She wants him to have some of Uncle's clothes and for me to choose a suit.

Had another very nice letter from Chris's wife. She sounds a dear. Shall be so glad when I have something to do.

Goodnight, dearest one.

13th May   10.20 pm

The longest week of my life, darling. I wonder if it has been ghastly for you, or I should say how ghastly.

Nothing to do all day. I washed and ironed a bit. Daddy got £40 for the radio you and I bet he would not get £30 and £35 for respectively!

I have just been kissing your photo, my baby. Darling, darling, darling.

The trunks with your clothes are in Stodge's flat. I am going up to get your tunic so that I can smell you. The smell upset me terribly when I was packing, but now I just long for it and don't care how sad it makes me. It's *you, you, you* I want. I can't think why God has let us go through all we have to be parted so soon. My head is splitting and my eyes all swollen with crying, so I must stop writing to you dearest and try and compose myself.

14th May   10.25 pm

Hallo, my darling. You must wonder why I am in bed at nearly the same time every night. It is because we go to bed just before black-out. Well, today is Sunday and after lunch, Daddy and I went to Bargie's. She had picked a very nice Glenurqhuart tweed suit for me and heaps of suits, trousers, etc. for Daddy. The things looked as if they had been tailored for him. She also gave me three cut-glass tankards and some old fish plates that have been in the family some years. Oh, and two very nice brass candlesticks Mummy had given Uncle. We had tea and got back at about 6.45 pm.

At 8 pm Judy Lockhart phoned and depressed me beyond words by telling me about some Australian pilot who had been with the main force the night you went missing and who saw nine *Path Finders* in trouble over Strasburg; two blew up with bomb loads on and seven were in flames. Oh dearest, I pray you are not badly burnt and suffering agonies. She tells me that on the last two occasions Guy went missing the first time she had news within one month and the second time, five days. Please God, we shall hear you are alright soon. I have just been saying my prayers and felt very comforted – I do so hope it is not just wishful thinking that has made me like that. Goodnight, my baby.

34

15th May   10.30 pm

Well, my darling, Daddy and I went up to Bargie's this morning to collect a heap of Uncle's clothes for Daddy. She was very nice and quite sane. We went on to Queen's Gate and dropped the things (tray, work-table, etc.) they were keeping at the shop for me there. Then on to Futofsky where I dropped Uncle's suit. He wants 12 guineas to make it and won't start for 3 months! Actually, he thinks it better for me to sell it. Have left it there for him to get a price.

Lunched with Stodge at a new place in Upper Regent Street called the Florida – lousy. Then went to see Isadore. He has not had an opportune moment to approach the firm but is doing so before the end of the week. Was very charming. Said your work would not take more than a day and half to two days to do, but they really wanted a showroom manageress or recep-tionist. Extraordinary thing – he sacked the girl whose name I can't remember, after ten years with them. I should think she was bitchy about their case and he overheard her remarks. It seems like provi-dence. He was so sweet because he was rather diffident about offering me the job. Said I could have a model girl and all that. To me it seems as if it is a job I can make anything of and when you come back I can either look after your customers when you bring them in or leave it and just keep house and cook for you darling, whichever you like. If I do work for the first three or four years after the war, it will be all the sooner for us to have a lovely farm in the country.

Oh, Georgie darling, I hope and pray you are not burnt and in pain. You can't think how awful this not knowing anything is, although I know how you will be worrying about what I am doing. When I have finished this I will try and concentrate and tell you I'm all right. It may help you. God gives me comfort after I have said my prayers. Oh don't let it be just wishful thinking. I took the snap of you and Ray to Wallace Heaton's today. I am having one of you alone and one of you together which I may send to Mrs Ridley because it is very characteristic of Ray.

A new offensive in Italy started yesterday and they have made a certain amount of progress. I should think they mean to do big things there before the middle of June when I imagine the Invasion will start. There was quite an amusing cartoon in the News tonight. A picture, headed 'Incredible', of a poor shivering little man walking down a wide lane all by himself with thousands of people either side of the lane, and underneath it says: 'The man who didn't have an Invasion Date?'

I wonder how many months it will be before you read this, darling.

Am going to concentrate on sending you my thoughts now, so goodnight my own husband.

16th May   11.35 pm

I am writing this later tonight, darling.

Dorrie and Bertie have been up to play solo. Had a letter from the Air Ministry this morning, telling me they are paying me £6 14s 3d per week. Don't know

whether they deduct income tax from that or not. Also
a letter from Toppy and a sweet one from Sal, saying
she hated leaving me alone and thought she should
come to me as I was getting a little absent-minded and
had sent her letter to Day. She evidently thinks her poor
old Mum is going off her rocker! Phoned Barbara
tonight as I had an idea from Lionel that she might
be up today. Am dining with her on Thursday night.
I don't think she'll think much of me not drinking.
She'll have to lump it. Really you know, darling, I have
become so used to it in the last 18 days, I don't miss
it very much. There are occasions when I am terribly
depressed when I would give quite a bit for a good
whisky and soda but then I think of my old darling
doing without and I'm thrilled that at least I can share
something with you – bless you, my own.

Spent the whole of today in the shop, helping Jean
mark off stuff Daddy bought in Brighton. I bought a
lovely oval gilt mirror for us. It will go beautifully over
the bureau or in our bedroom. I also bought a glass
jug with a part for ice – they couldn't sell it and had
reduced it from 29s 6d to 12s 6d. The mirror was 32s 6d
and worth about £4. Do hope you like it. If I write
as much as this every day and you don't come back for
6–7 months you will have a mass to get through. Do
hope it won't be too boring for you!

Should so like to meet Chris's wife. She sounds so nice
from her letters. I have just had such a strong feeling
that you are trying to tell me you are alive. I feel I want
to say 'Receiving you loud and clear, darling!' Am

longing to hear from Isadore, if they are going to take me on and when. I think it's in the bag. When I start I will try and arrange that one or two evenings a week I can go and pack parcels for the POW. Goodnight beloved, sleep well wherever you may be.

17th May   8.55 pm

Earlier tonight my poppet, Daddy and Jean have gone to a fire-watchers' lecture and I have just finished the washing up and seized this opportunity of writing to you. A fairly dull day. Posted parcels of sweets to the kids and did some washing. This afternoon Jean and I went to a sale at Hook. Jean bought a piano without Daddy having marked the catalogue! She paid £28 and Daddy says it's worth a fiver. Had a letter from Molly enclosing some peculiar form from the Red Cross about missing men. She had filled in the particulars for me. All wrong needless to say! Everyone seems to be treating me as if I have taken leave of my senses, I suppose because they all know how much I love you.

I wrote to Colin last week insuring the car against fire or theft and putting up the flat insurance to £1,000 and they had sent the account to Molly's! Only address they know now I have left Cambridge, I suppose. No cheque has arrived from Harrods (rent for flat). Nor have I had any letter from Gray, Son & Cook officially releasing me from the agreement over the lease. I wonder if they have taken the inventory yet.

I love you so much darling, the pain in my heart is agony. If only I could do something for you. It has thundered and rained and been bitterly cold today and I keep wondering if you are wandering across Europe in this awful weather. I think you must be a POW. Probably a better thing because you might so easily be killed by one of our own bombs in France at the moment.

Goodnight, dearest, shall have more to tell you tomorrow when I have seen Barbara.

18th May   11.05 pm   +*5s 8d*
A little more news tonight, beloved. This morning I went along to Gwen Brooks to see if she would pummel my tummy as now I am losing weight so rapidly it is hanging in more folds than ever. She is not qualified for abdominal massage, but she sent me to a lady osteopath called Miss Ritchie, a dour Scottish woman who is going to give me six treatments for 4 guineas. This afternoon I went to town and had my hair done and then met Barbara at the Mount Royal. She stood me dinner at l'Écu de France and I caught the 8.59 train home.

When I got home Cecilia was here! So I played solo and won 5s 8d I think. I will make a note by the date every day and so keep a tab on what I win and lose!

A cheque for £31 14s 3d came today from RAF – can't make out how they arrived at that. It seems to me too much to be my allowance and not enough to be your last month's pay. Must ask Bodger if it has been paid in. I shall pay all RAF cheques into your account, dearest, and then if I don't have to touch it, there will be a nice little daffy for when you come home and we celebrate! Oh, Georgie mine.

39

19th May   10.30 pm   +*5s*

Such a disappointment darling – I think Green
Hearns are quietly turning me down. I thought the job
was a cinch, but when I read the *Telegraph* this morning
they were advertising for a receptionist saleswoman. So,
I phoned Isadore at 9.30 am and asked him if he had
any news for me. He said, nothing very satisfactory, but
not to give up the idea completely, and to give him till
the beginning of next week. So I went to see Lionel and
asked him outright why they did not want me and he
said he did not know, he had not seen Isadore but would
do so tomorrow morning, Saturday, and find out and
tell me on Monday. I do hope they will not hire someone else in the meantime. I should think the old man
doesn't like me. Not flashy enough for them. I am
all right with Isadore, I'm sure. Oh, so what – I expect
there are plenty more jobs.

Tonight we have just played solo – for a change!
Three weeks today, my beloved and still no news.

I am wondering about the summer holidays, darling.
Think I shall try and take a little furnished place and
get hold of Nanny Dawes to look after the kids if I am
working. I told Lionel I was rather flabbergasted at
them turning me down, as it was a job I could do on
my back! I meant on my elbow, but of course he took
that up and never stopped pulling my leg. Said that
would be alright for Mr Hearn! I also said that you
had told me that if anything happened to you, I should
go to the firm, and they would give me a job. I said
it quite casually, in the middle of a conversation, but

I think it sank in. Well, dearest, on Monday I shall know the worst. Goodnight, my own darling boy.

20th May   12.30 pm   No cards

Rather late, darling – Daddy's birthday tomorrow, Sunday, so he took Jean, Cecilia and me to *Panama Hattie* and then on to the Ritz to dine. Saw Lionel there. What a wonderful show, darling, I was mad putting every one off it as I did. This morning, Daddy and I went in the car to Hampton Court to view some furniture. This afternoon, I paid my first visit to Miss Ritchie, the osteopath. She says most of that business we thought was glandular fever was muscular and one of the dorsal bones at the back of my neck is out of place. She thinks she can shift it later on when I have loosened up. As it was, she dragged me round the room by my neck. She says a lot of my fat is due to fluid and does not want me to drink much liquid – four cups per day maximum. She thinks she can do things to my tummy muscles. Apparently the shock of you going missing has made the muscles in my head, neck and shoulders go so taut, it is going to be a job to loosen them up.

It was hateful tonight, my beloved, without you. I kept thinking of the old man's birthday last year at the flat, when I trod on his glasses! And then coming down in the train, I thought of the night only a few weeks ago, when we went down with Muriel, Daddy, Jean and Mrs Jones and how cheerful we were. Everyone loves you so much, darling. Jean has at last changed me over to the single bed. I keep feeling for you in the night in the big one – it's hell, but how much worse it must be for you. Goodnight, best husband in the whole world – I adore you.

21st May   12 am   *+30s*

Absolutely no news today, my beloved. Daddy's birthday and we kept talking again about last year. I got up about noon. Did some exercises as prescribed by Miss R. Enormous lunch, during which I kept wondering what you were having to eat. Slept in the afternoon. Dorrie and Bertie up all the evening. Disgusted with me as I won 40s at solo, quite the most anyone has ever won at that game in this flat! I then proceeded to lose 10s at your funny little race game – 'Baccheroo'.

Tomorrow, I go to see Lionel and find out why the firm don't want me. Oh, Georgie, my darling, how much longer have I to suffer this awful suspense? Will you ever read this? Please God you will. Goodnight, my beloved. God bless and keep you safe wherever you are.

22nd May   12 am   *—15 11d*

A very eventful day, dearest. I went to see Lionel. Had a charming reception from him and Stephanie (she has been sweet). Lionel said he went across to Green Hearns on Saturday, but did not approach Isadore – presumably he saw the old man, and was told to mind his own business! So he was no further forward. So that was that. I then had an idea that I would take the bull by the horns and ask Marjorie Hughes her

42

advice and see if she could put in a word for me. I thought it would shake them all to the core if she championed me. She was charming, and got on the phone to Aubrey straightaway. Aubrey hummed and hawed and said they were considering me, but she knew how orthodox the old man is and he could not forget the divorce it seems. Anyway she left a message for Isadore to phone her. Then she had a brain wave. Apparently, there is a decent Jew whom you know called Cohen – marvellous stuff – sells to the wholesale and she has been trying to persuade him to open up a showroom in the West End. She phoned him, told him I knew all the West End buyers, could run the whole thing, etc. and he is quite enthusiastic and is going to see her about it. It's very decent of her, Georgie. But my word, she was quite hard on Stodge and you know how thick they were. I must mind my P's and Q's while this burst of friendliness lasts!

I do hope you think it was a good idea, putting one across the firm like that. They must be wondering at her *volte face*! She told me that Jane had told her all our side of the divorce question and she was disgusted that Don had not been man enough to let me divorce him and how sorry she was that the whole thing had been misrepresented to her in the first place. I was with her so long I had not time to see Bodger, but am taking her to lunch tomorrow and seeing him at 11.30. One thing I must tell you: Aubrey said to her that whatever happened they would not let down either of us financially. I thought it was pretty decent of them.

Now then for the most wonderful thing that happened in the middle of the night. Before I went to sleep I tried to get in touch with you mentally and failed. Suddenly, while I was sound asleep and not dreaming, it was like a shell bursting in my head and I got a message which said with no trimmings or endearments, 'I am alive, and trying to get home to you.' I was so shocked by it, it was so terrific I awoke at once. Oh, please, dear God it was not just brain strain and it really was a message God was good enough to let you get to me.

I pray every night, every morning – at all sorts of odd times during the day. I really believe God has been good to us and let you contact me last night.

Goodnight beloved. God bless you.

23rd May *–11d*

Went to Bodger at 11.30, darling. He was sweet and as the account was overdrawn £9, he must have been quite relieved to have had the cheque for £32 odd. Still have not had the rent from Harrods – devils.

Took Marjorie Hughes to lunch – it was her birthday, so she was quite pleased. She had called at Green Hearns but Aubrey and Isadore were both out. The old man was most reticent about the job and said it rested with the boys. Mr Cohen phoned her again this morning and seemed quite enthusiastic about the scheme. She says she will put all her business through me as the prices will then suit her better. He is going to see her this week. She says she would like the job herself. Saw Miss Coy for some orange skin cream and she was sweet and hopes you will come home soon.

Letter from Hugh. Has been recommended for promotion to captain. Suppose it is about time really. Must write and tell him about you. I feel full of confidence tonight, darling. Sleep well, wherever you are and God bless you. I adore you.

24th May   11.30 pm – All square

A lousy day, dear heart, nothing to do but mope around and worry about you. In the morning I went round to all the chemists trying to buy blackcurrant purée for Marjorie Hughes. She is lacking in vitamin C since she had the baby. Do hope she gets cracking on this job for me – it is obvious Green Hearns are not having me.

Barbara phoned today. She told me among other things she had lunch with Lionel a few months ago and he was going on about the divorce. I never thought our private affairs would have such an effect on the business world!

Viewed some furniture this afternoon. Went to lousy film at the Élite, *Fallen Sparrow*. Cecilia came to dinner and has just gone. Won 2s 6d from Daddy; he bet me 'fetid' was spelt 'feted'. Money for jam!

Georgie, my darling husband, how long are you going to be away from me? Where are you? I pray you are not badly burnt, those wounds want so much care. I wish I could help you somehow, darling. No one can guess quite what this hell I am in is like. Knowing nothing, perfectly helpless and trying, trying, trying not to let my imagination run away with me. Goodnight, my own man. God bless and keep you.

25th May   10.15 pm

Bad news of Kenneth, darling, in the *Evening News* tonight. So terribly disappointing, as on the Saturday following the news you were missing, the boys who came over from Oakington said his bomb aimer's wife had had a card saying he was a POW. Another terrible day.

Bonsor's sale this afternoon, solo tonight. Hal Lawson phoned just now to tell me the numbers of the Swiss planes had come through! I told him I knew but thought it might hurt his feelings if I told him I had known a week afterwards, especially as I want him to keep me informed.

So depressed tonight, my beloved. I have to keep looking at your photo and saying 'Come on, Pip, chin up.' Have made enquiries today about a sickness policy. Think it would be good in case I get any funny illness, and also phoned Bodger and told him to buy £20 worth of saving certificates every month. If your account is not going to be used, my allowance from the Air Ministry covers the never-nevers and Green Hearn's can be invested. Your money may as well work while it is waiting for you. What I can't understand, darling, is why Cyril Evans' £5 was cancelled last October when it should have gone on for 20 months! Bodger says let sleeping dogs lie and if he does not write for it, don't

46

worry: you may have had a bet with him or something.
So what. You're a wicked old devil and I adore you.
Hurry up and come back to me. Goodnight, sweet-
heart.

26th May   10.15 pm (Left money on table!)

Oh, darling, I've just made an awful fool of myself.
Dorrie's been up playing cards. I have felt so miserable
all day and Daddy started one of his silly arguments.
I couldn't stand it and just got up and screamed at him
and walked out screaming. So now I am in bed having
made a bloody fool of myself. My nerves just all went
to pieces. Oh, darling, it's so much worse for you, I must
try and keep that in the front of my mind.

I have been to town today and made my will with
Landau. I can't write any more, darling, am crying all
over the page. Oh, Georgie mine, this is absolute
torture. Where are you?

27th May   Whit Sunday   —42s

Afraid I was somewhat incoherent last night, my
poppet. Must have got my nerves all tangled up! Apolo-
gised to everyone concerned today anyway. Went to
Hampton with Daddy this morning. Cinema with him
and Jean in the afternoon, *A Bloke Called Jo*. Not bad.
Solo with Dorrie tonight. Kitty was very big as I
doubled at *25s* so we went on playing till 12.30.

Don't think I told you I had a very nice letter from
Dickey one day this week. His wife and babe are at Cot-
tenham so perhaps he has Cap's place.

I expect this writing book and case will be pretty greasy by the time I have finished as I always write while my face cream is soaking in. What a useless sort of life I am leading at the moment, it seems so futile but I really can't rush into a job and I don't want to take on a house or flat of my own till I know a bit more where I am. Wouldn't it be wonderful if the Air Ministry phoned in the morning to say you were at Gib? O my darling, I must not think of anything like that, goodnight, God bless you, and keep you safe.

28th May   Sunday   10.45 pm   +9s 1d

Another dragging day darling. Terribly hot. I was lazy, stayed in bed till noon. Had lunch, read and wrote letters in the afternoon. I have advertised Uncle's suit in the *Lady* for 16 guineas! Two pairs of trousers made me put the price fairly high. I have decided if I get that, it will be cheaper for me to have a new suit. As Futofsky is charging 20 guineas now, that will only be 4 guineas to pay, whereas if I have the other converted he will charge about 12 guineas making. Tonight we played the everlasting solo. I don't know whether I shall be able to stand much more of it.

People on leave must be having a heavenly weekend, darling. It is Whitsun and just the weather you like. I don't feel very hopeful today, darling. Oh, please God, you are alive and well, my beloved. How long will I have to wait to know? 30 days so far. I must try not to be sorry for myself, when you are probably hungry and hellishly uncomfortable. Goodnight, dearest. God bless you.

29th May   Whit Monday   11.35 pm   +5s

A better day, darling. Jean, Daddy and I got on a train to Oxshott and took a picnic lunch. You would have loathed it. Crowds of people on the train, and there when we arrived. We had to look for a tree without anyone underneath it! Jean had been the one who was so keen to go and she grumbled non stop all the time! The ground was too hard, there were too many insects, she couldn't find the food she wanted in the blasted carrier, and eventually we caught the 3.55 back! Tonight we have played solo with Dorrie; Daddy and Jean have argued and quarrelled all the time. Wardle is coming tomorrow to do up the lounge so we have been moving all the furniture about.

Sally went to Pulborough for the weekend and back today. John is still at home; he has had pneumonia and now he is ready to return, but the school has German measles. Goodnight, my darling, darling, darling.

30th May   Tuesday   11 pm   −2s

This morning Jean went to town and Daddy and I went to a sale at Hampton. We went by car and on the way there got behind a dirty old Ford which reminded me of ours and I distinguished myself by bursting into tears! Did some washing this afternoon and washed my hair tonight, then played solo. Bargie phoned and was so cheerful about you and seemed to have a hunch that I should get good news. She is such a funny old stick, I believe she might be right. She has given me some brass candlesticks, a watch Gran won for swimming and a cocktail shaker. We did want one, so that's very acceptable. When I go to town tomorrow I will call on Westley, pay him for that last lot of drink we had, and see if I can get some more to pack away till you get back. So far I have two bottles of gin (one from Miss Smith!) and two half bottles of whisky I got from Curtis before I left.

By the way, today is the 30th and I still have not heard from Gray, Son and Cook as to how much I owe them and how much they owe me for coke. Shall let sleeping dogs lie. Day says in her letter this morning her glands are up behind her knees. I wonder what on earth can be the matter with her. I suppose the pathologist who took the blood test the time before last knew what he was doing.

Goodnight, my baby, I feel ridiculously hopeful tonight. Here's praying and hoping. God bless you. I love you so.

31st May   Wednesday   11 pm   +5s 2d

It is the end of the month, and now 33 days without you, my darling husband.

Today I went to town. Saw Landau about my will, he had got a draft out but nothing to sign. I hope I have done the right thing. I have left my jewellery and the £1,000 Watney Coombe and Reid Shares to the children and everything else to you, darling, making you executor with Daddy and Charles Shuter. Hope you think that is all right. After Landau, lunched with Vi at Derry's and tried to get a black frock from her – she didn't have one. Then saw Marjorie Hughes. She had another idea about me going to Needhams. Then home and solo once again – just for a change! Good-night, dearest, God bless and keep you safe.

JUNE

1st June   Thursday   10.50 pm   +*15*

Nothing much to tell you today, darling. Had a pain in my tummy and got up late. Went across to the shop and typed a letter to Jo Needham suggesting he might like to re-open a West End showroom which I could manage. A good letter, I think you would have approved. Did Jean's shopping and this afternoon helped her spring clean all the lounge furniture. We have changed over the china cabinet with the bookcase – a *great* improvement. I have hidden those awful water colours and the room looks twice the size. If we can only get Daddy used to it without them, it will be all right They are both being so very good to me, Georgie darling. I am so terribly strung up. I try very hard not to let myself go and they do understand remarkably well. But you don't know how I long to be alone with the children. Not by myself because my thoughts frighten me, but just with my babies till you come back to me. Oh, Georgie, when shall I get any news. It would be heaven to go to bed knowing definitely that you were still in the world with me and to go to sleep without crying. I am a baby I know, but it is the only time I get to myself and I cry for you and pray for you every night, my beloved.

The snap of you and Ray is specially good of you,

darling, and so often cheers me. It is just as if you are saying, 'Chin up, Pippy darling, of course I'm coming back to you!' Next week will be six weeks, dearest. I wonder if that is still too soon to hope for news.

Goodnight, my darling. Such a big kiss.

2nd June   7.30 pm

Very early to bed tonight, dearest, I have such a splitting headache. I went to bed this afternoon. Muriel and I are taking Sally for a picnic tomorrow. She has not been to Liss at all yet and wants to go. So I went to Kingston this morning to get some food. Managed four baby lobsters from Sam and asparagus from Barney who insisted on me going to the Griffin and having a beer with him! There was a priceless card from Chris Lucas this morning for us, this is what it said:

W.C.
L.W. 30.5.44

M.D.P & G.
     H.A.Y?
     D.Y.E.C.T.W?
     W.S.M.L.T.S.Y
     H.C.A.   O.K.

L
F&C

I was shaken to the core when I saw it, but it did not

take long to decipher. Have been meaning to write to them for sometime and kept on forgetting.

In the *Evening News* tonight there is an article on a train load of bombs which blew up in Cambridgeshire so Daddy is full of fifth columnists tonight. Just as well I am in bed or I should be rude I am afraid.

Did I tell you he wrote to Scotland Yard the other day because while he was in Frank's hairdresser in Piccadilly, someone came in with boxes containing thousands of sixpences and shilling pieces? Poor detectives, as if they haven't enough to do. The laundry arrived from Cambridge today, an enormous parcel which I must undo and check I suppose. My head feels as if it is going to crack, back and front.

I wonder how many of these books I shall fill before you come home, darling and if you will ever bother to read them. I feel that you will think it a good thing, my darling and you will know what I am doing every day you are away from me. Cecilia is here tonight so they have someone to play solo with. I tried at Bentalls to get a Major Hoyles so that we could perhaps get the rules right but they haven't one. Shall try at Selfridges sometime. Should have gone to my osteopath today but had too bad a pain. Going next Wednesday. If I put that here I shall be able to look it up.

11 pm +7s 6d Dragged out for a game of solo after all, darling, and as my last thoughts are always of you had to write another line to tell you. Goodnight, and God bless you.

3rd June   Saturday   10.20 pm   +*4s 8d*

A lovely day with Sally. Muriel and I met at Surbiton station at 10 am and caught the 10.13. Arrived at school about noon where Sal and Christine were waiting for us. The picnic was terribly heavy so we just walked into the woods opposite the heather part where we picnicked on strawberries last summer. Then after the kids had eaten themselves to a standstill we caught a bus to Petersfield where we went from one chemist to another buying Ovaltine tablets, then to the Punch and Judy where we went last time, then bus back to school. The gardener, Draper, insisted upon giving me half a dozen lettuces to take home, so I dropped 2s and we then took our taxi to the station in time to catch the 5.57 pm back to Surbiton. Got in about 7.15, supper and solo. A letter from Nig asking me to meet her for tea on the 15th when she is coming up for a fitting, and a note from Jays to say my *Path Finder* badge is ready. Also cheque from the Air Ministry for £28 18s 5d. Wish I knew how they worked it out. I suppose it must be free of income tax. They always deduct at source, don't they?

There was a paragraph in the *Evening News* this week saying the Germans are not broadcasting the names of any more prisoners. I hope that does not mean they are going to hold back names from the Red Cross. I have waited long enough and you must be worrying yourself sick about letting me know. Wouldn't it be wonderful if I had a card from you yourself tomorrow, beloved? Goodnight, and God keep you safe for me.

4th June   Sunday   1.45 pm   —2s 1d

Very sad tonight, darling, just can't help missing you
so desperately and keep thinking I may never see you
again on earth, it's ghastly. This morning I went up
to Muriel's to get Stodge's flat keys, as I wanted to get
a thermos out of the storebox (I bust Jean's at the picnic
yesterday, filled it full of ice and must have pressed it
in too tight!) Had lime juice with Muriel, back to lunch
and then Jean and I met Muriel at the station and went
to the pictures together! Funny combination.

Played solo tonight and felt so unhappy I hardly
knew how to contain myself. Come back to me my
beloved, come back, Georgie mine. I can't go on without you. I had a lovely lovely dream about us, just you
and me early this morning, I woke up having nearly forgotten for a second. I am longing to go to sleep and see
if I can dream of you again. This is about the first time
and I have tried so hard. Seems so extraordinary when
you are never, never out of my thoughts for a moment.

The fifth and eighth armies will be in Rome by
tomorrow. Our bombardment of all invasion ports and
railway junctions this week has been terrific and the
Americans have started their shuttle service to Russia,
bombing on the way out, landing in Russia, re-loading
and bombing on the return journey. So it looks as if
everything is about all set for the invasion. There is such
a terrible drought in England, I wonder how on earth
we are going to feed Europe and ourselves this coming
winter. If it does not rain soon, crops will be ruined.
I don't know whether these odd bits I am telling you

will be of any interest to you, dear heart. I hope so. God bring you back soon. Goodnight, beloved.

5th June 8 pm Monday +*3s 7d*

Hello, my poppet. Daddy and Jean have gone to the pictures, so I have been writing a few letters including one to Bodger enclosing the Air Ministry cheque. Then I thought it would be a good opportunity to write to you, my darling. This morning I had my hair permed at the ends, and this afternoon went over to Wimbledon to see Madame Jean. She was sweet, is going to make me a black frock for every day. Says if I want to start on my own she will always back me and work for me wherever I am.

I picked up an RAF brooch in the road today, do hope it means good luck, darling. Have just been on the phone to Judy Lockhart. She is working at the American Red Cross in Colchester.

You know, darling, I think I was numbed at first by shock, because now the pain gets worse and worse every day. I must stop being sorry for myself. Poor boy, if you are a prisoner I know how unhappy you will be. It is what you have always dreaded. No dreams of you last night. Perhaps I shall be luckier tonight.

I have smoked a whole box of Abdullas in two weeks! So today I bought myself ten Salisburys and am going to try and get used to them. I must write to Hugh, I have not told him about you yet. I got some air mail letters today when I was in the post office changing our threepenny bits into five Saving Certificates! Everyone seems so short of pennies it is difficult not to spend a threepenny bit now and then!

10.45 pm. They wanted an hour's solo after they came in, so we played and I won 3s 7d. So unhappy tonight, dearest – no hope left.

Goodnight and God bless you, beloved man.

6th June   Tuesday   11.30 pm   _D Day_   *— 3s 6d*

Well, my darling, Invasion Day at last! I wonder if you know, wherever you are. Landings were made in Normandy about 7.30 am this morning after Bomber Command had bombed invasion ports, etc. all night. Since midnight today 31,000 airmen have been over France! 7,500 sorties. About nine this morning the Supreme Commander was issuing orders to Belgium, Holland, France, etc. Churchill said in the Commons tonight that massed air landings behind the enemy line in France had been successful. He also says we have 11,000 First Line planes to call on and 4,000 ships. Thousands of smaller vessels crossed the Channel this morning and the resistance was not as heavy as had been expected. Fighting seems to have been fiercest at Caen.

I am writing this in the lounge. Daddy and Jean have gone to bed so I thought I would take the opportunity of writing to you on a table for a change, and let you know a few of the headlines in case you don't get any news where you are. Poor old poppet, this is just what you and Kenneth were looking forward to.

This morning I went to town to collect my _Pathfinder_ badge and sundry watches, and paid the drink bill.

Spent rest of the afternoon with Bargie, who was not quite so mad as usual and took me to dinner at 6.30 to a restaurant opposite Belle Meunière. Had quite a good dinner and she was very sweet. Brought home the cocktail shaker and candlesticks and Gran's watch. All very nice, but she insisted on me having an awful looking mirror for which Uncle had carved the frame. Didn't like to hurt her by refusing.

I got home to hear the King's speech at 9 pm. He was very hesitant to start with but quickened half way through. Even so, a speech is not interesting unless it flows easily and his was rather difficult to piece together. As far as I could gather he called the Nations to prayer and said how the Queen sympathised with the women of the country who kept vigil for their men.

The weather is not too good. It is extremely windy and cold. The invasion was postponed 24 hours because of that. All I hope is that this means you will get home quicker than ever, dearest.

Time for news:

New communique from Supreme HQ has not arrived and it is now 12.21, so they are playing the interval signal for dear life. Pretty decent of them to stay on the air. I suppose so many millions are waiting for it. I wonder if you can hear it anywhere. I don't suppose so as I think you must be a prisoner, my poor baby. Nothing much in the second communique, only a resumé of what we already know. Oh, boy, what's the good of it all without you?

Goodnight, dear heart. God bless you.

7th June   Wednesday   11.15 pm   +*13s*

The phone went at 7.45 this morning dearest, I got so excited, I thought it might be news of you but no, it was Marjorie Hughes. She had had lunch the previous day with Cecil Cohen of Alfred Cohens and he wants to open up in the West End again. She said did I mind going back into frocks, so I said I didn't. Tonight I rang her and she said Cecil had phoned to say he had called a board meeting for tomorrow and wanted to see me as soon as they had had it. He says you and I had a drink with him a few months ago, I am afraid I don't remember him, but Marjorie says he is quite a nice little Jew.

This morning I went to Miss Richie and felt dreadful when I came out. Typed an agreement with Daddy's Duncan Terrace landlords for him. Went with him to Kingston to view Bonsors. This afternoon being early closing, Jean and Cecilia went to the pictures. I retired to bed feeling like hell and Daddy went to sleep. Tonight we played the everlasting solo. Had a letter from a Mrs Johnstone, mother of your young Sergeant Engineer. Very sweet, poor darling. He is their only child and such a baby.

With regard to the second front. We flew 13,000 sorties yesterday and the Hun is cleared off the beaches. I should imagine the fighting proper will start tomorrow. De Gaulle is in London at last and addressed France yesterday. I don't think I told you that.

It's funny darling, that when you are in a hole or looking for a job, it is all the unexpected people who help you. Here is Marjorie determined to get me fixed up before she goes for her holiday on Sunday and yet Vi has not got a single idea, she can only suggest advertising! Letter from Miss Nagel this morning saying Sally was thrown from her pony on Sunday and they were keeping her quiet for a week. I phoned at 8.30 and she said they did not know how it happened. She was apparently galloping, came off, picked herself up and went home, then said she felt rotten. They got the doctor to examine her and he says there are no signs of concussion but is keeping her in bed for the week. So I hope there is nothing to worry about. I must try and get down today or Saturday.

I think Daddy and I may go to a sale at Farnham tomorrow. I've got a glimmer of hope again today, my darling. Oh the heavenly heavenly relief if I hear you are alive and coming home to me.

Goodnight, darling. God bless you.

8th June   Thursday   12.30 am   *+18s 9d*

Daddy and I set off for Farnham at 8.30 this morning. I quite enjoyed the day. The sale was in the garden and it was sunny. The only thing that was not so good was that while the bidding was at its height, the auctioneer suddenly said, 'Is Mr Martin of Surbiton here? He is wanted on the phone urgently.' Well, of course I immediately thought it was something to do with you, darling. Daddy went in to the house to answer the phone and they locked the front door after him. So there was I left shivering with fright on on the step. And then, after all that, it was only Jean, who had got the wind up about some furniture from Teddington which had not turned up at the shop! Phew, was I relieved when he told me. Even then I did not believe it for a few minutes and thought he was keeping something from me.

As regards the second front. The Germans are counter-attacking with their reserves and being held off! The beach heads are all over and we have taken Bayeaux, where the inhabitants greeted us with open arms, flowers, wine, etc. Rather interesting to find out what our first reception by the French would be like.

Since Tuesday we have flown 27,000 sorties and lost 289 aircraft! The Germans have lost 178. Last night Bomber Command lost 29 on targets round Paris and Cherbourg. A bit much, I think. Our paratroops have been well equipped with all necessary armaments, and reserves were flown up today.

When will you be with me, darling? Wish I could have a peep into the future, because I don't want to go on without you. God bless, darling, it's very late.

9th June   Friday   11.15 pm   +5d

A letter from Sal this morning, darling. I think she has been worse than Nags made out. She talks about not knowing she had been out with me the previous day when she *eventually* came round at 10.30 on *Sunday night* and that Matron had a mattress in her bedroom that night. I phoned Nags and she still says there is nothing to worry about. Anyhow I have written asking her to get the doctor to overhaul her again before she gets up again, and for Matron to keep a look out for aches and pains. She was apparently dragged for quite a way.

This morning I did all my washing and the whole of the rest of the day I worked in the shop. I forgot to tell you, I bought an entrée dish the same pattern as ours at the Farnham sale for 45s. Today I bought two lovely goblets for 3s 6d the pair and six finger bowls (useful for hors d'oeuvres) for 9s. I phoned Marjorie Hughes today, she had not heard from Cecil Cohen as to when he wanted to see me, but says not to worry as the board meeting was only yesterday and he had definitely said he wanted to see me before anyone else. Seems to have been impressed at this first meeting which I can't remember, can you? Says he remembered me as a very stylish woman! As she goes away on Sunday, it is a nuisance I have to make the appointment through her. I suppose having waited six weeks (today) I can wait another two for work.

Am going to see Day tomorrow. I have asked Miss Robley Brown to let her borrow a bike and meet me at the station at Great Missenden, tomorrow. As it has poured all day long I don't think a picnic will be much good, so am going early to try and book some lunch. Didn't we have a funny lunch somewhere near there once?

Everyone is amazed that I have stuck to no drink and do you know, darling, it honestly *does not mean a thing to me*. I only want to drink with you. Life is so wonderful when we are together and so completely colourless without you, dear heart.

I love you, love you so desperately. Goodnight, beloved. God bless you.

10th June   Saturday   10.30 pm   *+5s 8d*

You'll laugh at me, darling, but I long for this time every night, when I feel I am alone with my thoughts of you. Judy Lockhart phoned tonight. She was miserable as it is Guy's birthday today. I caught a train from Marylebone and arrived at Great Missenden about 11.50. Went all round the town to try and get lunch but it was impossible. The pub we went to last time had a cricket party, and everywhere else was full. Eventually found a pub called the George where they gave us lovely soup, sandwiches and coffee and biscuits. After lunch we caught a train to Aylesbury, went to the pictures and had tea. Day looked quite well and has lost some weight which is good.

As far as the second front is concerned, we are holding our own, digging in and have taken 4–5,000 prisoners. Our troops are trying to take the Cherbourg Peninsula, I think, and then go on to the Channel Islands.

How much longer before news of you comes through, my beloved? I have felt more hopeful the last two days. Not that it means anything really. Oh Georgie you *must* be safe somewhere, darling. Goodnight, sweetheart.

11th June   Sunday   11.15 pm   *—18s 6d*

Did not get up till 12.30. Cecilia came to lunch. Went to pictures this afternoon and saw *Hatters Castle*. Quite good. I don't really think it spoilt the book, which most films do. Then we played solo till just now; a dreadfully dull day. I have been trying to find out if there is a local Red Cross for sending parcels to POWs. But everyone seems to think I shall be popped on the labour exchange books if I apply to help, specially as I have not got a job yet. Should so hate a factory, darling. So I suppose I must go on helping Daddy as best I can.

I wonder if there will be news of you this week, darling. The Germans have flooded part of Normandy, from one to seven feet in parts. Otherwise things seem to be going quite well. The front is about 51 miles wide and 11 deep in parts. Men had letters from home actually on D Day on the beaches. In Italy our armies are 50 odd miles past Rome and going like mad. On the Russian front things seem quiet and have been for some weeks. Goodnight and God bless you, my beloved.

12th June   Monday   10.30 pm   +5s 8d

This morning I had two answers to my advert in *The Lady* (about Uncle's suit). One was from a Dr Snellen at 17 Berkley Street. So I took it there this morning after phoning. It turned out to be the Dutch Colonial Offices. Quite a nice old man; I hope it fits him. He is letting me know tomorrow.

I went to the osteopath in the afternoon; there is no doubt she has loosened me up marvellously and you would not recognise my tummy, it is so nice and flat (and my botty). I called at Futofskys to pick up the suit. The old man is very poorly. Esther had some undies to sell minus coupons. She wanted £8 for pure silk camiknickers and £4 for artificial silk which looked worth about 19/11!! I got out as gracefully as possible. I must have some new undies soon, though. My poor nighties have had such a shock at suddenly being worn again it has completely shattered them! I am in rags.

I love you, so, darling, and am missing you so terribly. Sometimes I dare to think that we shall be together on earth again one day and then I think it is too much to hope for and perhaps this is the way I have to pay for taking you from your first wife. Please, dear God that you come back to me. I can't live without you, Georgie mine. Goodnight, darling.

13th June   Tuesday   9.30 pm   *+6s 9d*

Three years ago today, darling, I met a gentleman on the six o'clock train at Paddington from Plymouth!! You, my beloved, returned from the Middle East. All day today I have thought I might have had news and now I am so terribly depressed I have been, and am, crying my heart out as I write. One minute I wish I could die, then I think you may be alive somewhere and all I want on earth is to be with you.

Have come to bed early because Daddy and I have been quarrelling. He has had about three drinks and is being stupid and horrible – seems more so to me I suppose, as I don't drink.

This morning there was a letter from Pam Rowlie who had been to the Air Ministry and heard about you. Dr Snellen phoned to say he was delighted with the suit, and the cheque was in the post (hope it is). Daddy and

I went to Weybridge to view furniture and then on to another viewing at Wimbledon this afternoon. A game of cards – a row and so to bed. Oh, I want you, want you, want you. You would never have let me get cross with Daddy.

I must stop thinking about myself and try and remember something about the second front to tell you.

Our Air forces flew 14,000 sorties. Sorry *bombers*, goodness knows how many fighter planes were out. Naughty old Churchill crossed to Normandy in the Kelvin and was over there being literally mobbed by the boys for seven hours. He has guts at his age. Thank God nothing happened to him. The front is now over 60 miles wide and in parts 18½ miles deep. The Cherbourg Peninsula is nearly cut through. In fact things are pretty good all round. In Italy we are 70 miles past Rome. Russia is giving Finland hell. The Luftwaffe has still failed to do much. Our Lancs were out last night and I think we lost 17. The papers say that the German planes are being kept for defence of the Reich and that Munich is a hot bed of fighters. At the moment I feel as if I can't stay in this bloody little flat another minute. I should love to go to Fred and Mabel for a day or two but am afraid I should cry in front of everyone who asked how you were. Goodnight, dearest. God keep you.

14th June   Thursday   11.15 pm   +*14s*

A better day, dearest, This morning we had arranged that Daddy should go to the Wimbledon sale and Jean and I to Weybridge. At 9.15 she had a phone call from her mother in a frightful stew. Apparently Billy, Jean's nephew, had been given a lot of radio parts by an American airforce chap and had sent them home. He has now discovered they were stolen and the authorities are trying to trace them! Jean went to town to see her mother so I went to Weybridge on my own. Quite enjoyed it though the stuff fetched awful prices and I only spent £18 odd. I talked to a dear old boy who was one of the dealers. He had lost his wife in a blitz and four of his shops and was trying to keep going – I should think he had really retired. Showed me photos of three grandsons in RAF, Army and Navy. The navy boy was only 15 and had been torpedoed twice!

A letter from Nags to say the doctor had examined Sal and she was OK, but not working for a couple of days. Quite a good thing I think. Also had the cheque for Uncle's suit. 2,000 heavies out between dawn and midday today and goodness knows how many fighters. The front is now 75 miles wide and 20 deep. We have heard very heavy gunfire tonight, sounds miles away so we don't know whether it's coastal, or Hitler's secret weapon.

Six weeks and five days since you started for Friedrichshafen, darling. Oh, I do hope and pray I have good news this week. Goodnight, my husband. May God keep and protect you, beloved.

15 June   Thursday   10.30 pm   —3s

So tired tonight, dearest. Shopped with Jean this morning and this afternoon walked from shop to shop round the West End trying to find Day a suit, so that it is ready for her to try on Saturday morning when she is coming up to town for the day. Met Nig and Katie at Marshall's for tea. I found some lovely *petit point* chair seats in the cushion department – they had come off a liner which had been dismantled, 9s 6d for the small ones, 12s 6d the large. It was closing time when I found them, so I am going back tomorrow. Nig and Katie went off to Liverpool Street early because of the Derby crowds – which is this Saturday. Nig tells me they are on their third CO since Guy at Oakington. They must have been having a lousy time.

The girl whose husband was missing, opposite us in Hills Avenue – Joan Robinson – heard he was a prisoner in eight weeks. Perhaps we shall be lucky next week. Goodnight beloved, no more now, I can hardly keep my eyes open. God bless you, my own.

16th June   Friday   10.15 pm

Last night the pilotless planes started their games. I am afraid I upset the family by not waking up sufficiently to discuss every bomb they heard. Morrison broadcast at 11 this morning to say that they had been over the South of England. Parliament are not giving away districts as it might help the Germans to adjust them. We have had alerts on and off all day and there was one tonight at 9.30. Daddy and Jean are fire-watching, which means they have to go to the shelter at the alert. As the 'All Clear' did not go till about 9 am this morning they should have a good time!

I went to town this morning and bought the tapestry seats I told you about, six small ones for backs, six larger for seats, all for £6 17s 6d. They were very difficult to pick out as some were a bit moth-eaten. I have sent them to the cleaners and shall now have to look out for chairs for them to go on! I know you will love them and they will look grand against our pink carpet. I stood behind Charles Hopwood in a queue for taxis at Waterloo this morning. The bloody fool asked me if I had ever married you, after I told him you were missing. I went into Shuter Fashions and told Carol the only suit I could get for Day was about £12 15s 10d and let her know I had walked miles looking for one. I meet Day at Baker Street at 10.40 tomorrow and shall take her to lunch at the Hungaria. I phoned Vecchi and told him about you as I could not bear them all to ask me how you are – as they always do if I go in on my own.

I had a lovely letter from Margaret Martin today. I think she must have a sense of humour and feel a bit like me too, by the things she said in it. She said she was afraid she gave Janie an awful shock as she told her about you in the most casual manner, as if she lost husbands and friends every day. That is just the way I have to tell people for fear I burst into tears.

Daddy and Jean are both a bit tired and Daddy distinctly irritable tonight after a bad night fire-watching. Goodness knows what he will be like tomorrow if they are up fire-watching again tonight. I wonder how terribly thin you are, darling? I seem to have stopped losing weight just lately, although Nig and Katie noticed a tremendous difference in me.

Goodnight, beloved, may God bless and keep you. Do you know darling, I have to try so hard not to bargain with God in my prayers every night. I find myself promising all sorts of things if only He will let you come back to me safely. I know how you would tease me, but I do feel we shall both be better people for this ghastly time darling, when we do eventually get together again, don't you?

17th June   Saturday   10 pm   —3s 1d

Hello, dearest, quite a nice day with Day. These bloody Robot planes (will call them RPs in future) have been about all day and night. Daddy and Jean were up all night so I must do their fire-watching next time. Day and I went straight to Pontings where Miss Jarvis let me have a very nice West of England tweed suit for £5. Fitted Day beautifully, except the skirt which was too long. Then to the Hungaria for lunch. Vecchi was sweet. We had lovely hors d'oeuvres, hot lobster thermidor and delicious sweets and he made a tremendous fuss of us. He and Dessi both took us up to the table and were so attentive. Afterwards Carol wanted to see Day, so we went to a News Reel then I gave her over to Carol and asked her to get the skirt altered. On the way back to Surbiton these bloody little planes were bursting on all sides of the train. Didn't hurt anyone but cracked glass and filled the carriages with dust. They just missed the line in each case. I cooked a beautiful soufflé omlette stuffed with chopped ham and onions tonight, darling, Jean was feeling tired. I thought how much you would have loved it.

Today was Derby Day and I backed the winner along with three others! Still, it was 28–1 so at 2s 6d each way, I win about £3 12s 6d, I think (just worked it out again).

I wonder if we shall be together next Derby Day darling, or if I am going to be on my own all my life? Oh, please not, I want you so much. Goodnight, beloved. May God guard you and bring you safely back to me.

18th June   Sunday   10.15 pm   *+2s 9d*

Phew! what a night. Even I couldn't sleep a wink. RPs coming over all night long and our barrage simply terrific. Shrapnel thudding on the roof all the time but none came through, thank goodness. People seem to be taking them pretty calmly as far as I can make out, all except Jean who gets into such a flap and ought to try not to.

In Normandy the Americans have cut through the Cherbourg Peninsular which I believe bottles up about 25–30,000 Germans in the tip. The weather has not been too good across the Channel so not much air activity. The French Maquis or Patriots have done an amazing amount of sabotage in occupied France and the Vichy bosses are in a jam.

I do hope these bits will be of interest to you, dearest, but if you are in a prison, you are bound to miss it or hear wrong accounts aren't you?

We did not get up till 11.30 this morning after our ghastly night. Then to The Wagon (I had two Bass and felt really light headed!). Lunch at three, more sleep till seven. Just your sort of Sunday, my own. Oh, if only I could put my arms round you now and kiss that darling curly head. Goodnight, darling, sleep well.

19th June   Monday   11.45 pm   *+3s 10d*

What a dreadful night, darling. They stopped firing at the RPs as they came in. I counted and saw 28 explode. It was uncanny not hearing the guns and I did not sleep nearly so well as when it is noisy. Jean is in such a state of jitters, Daddy is taking her away the day after tomorrow, so I shall go to Mabel and Nig for a few days I think, if I can arrange for the post to be sorted out.

There was a letter from Daddy Ridley this morning asking for news of you and saying the Group Captain had sent Ray's gun by a passing lorry. Think the nerves of my tummy have gone to hell. I was up all night and feel as if I shall be tonight. So silly, when I think of you.

This afternoon Daddy and I went to a sale at Hampton Court. It was not up to much so we spent the afternoon at the Palace! When we returned to the shop a woman had called and said she wanted to sell the contents of her house at Tolworth. It was one which had been blasted to bits on Saturday morning. We had a very difficult time wading through broken glass and plaster trying not to go through the wall into the next house. How Daddy managed to price the stuff I don't know. The poor woman was nearly off her head and kept telling me she had not had her clothes off for a week, but it happened on Saturday and today's only Monday. She spoke so well of the Rest Centre where they had fed and slept her, said they could not do enough for the people. Two whole roads were pretty well smashed with that Saturday morning. Jean just missed one outside Catesbys this morning. It was her cinema day with her mother and one dropped in Tottenham Court Road just as she moved away from Catesbys, and turned a bus over with 40 people in it.

I am so Georgie sick, God Bless and keep you, my own.

20th June   Tuesday   11 pm   +1s 9p

Guildford all day with Daddy, dear heart. Things were fetching awful prices, so we did not buy much. I bought a white feather boa for 10s. I thought it would look nice on a negligé for when you come home. We met Elaine in the High Street with her little boy, a peeky, white faced child and thin with an old man's face. I had a letter from Sally saying she was not at school yet and could not play games as she got such awful headaches. I think Miss Nagel makes rather light of these things. I should like to get in touch with the doctor myself tomorrow.

Jean and Daddy have gone down to the shelter: she is windy and he is fire-watching. Actually of course with the buggers dropping all round us it is the right thing to do, but I could not face sleeping in a pokey garage, with a crowd of smelly women, children and animals!

Do you know Georgie, in spite of my having put up the insurance on the flat to £1,000 I don't believe we have ever paid war risk on it! I really must phone Colin tomorrow and find out. When Nig was up the other day I asked her to be good enough to have the Ford put on blocks and take the battery to a garage to have it charged. I believe that is the right procedure and we shall want to have a holiday with it as soon as you come home!

Today I felt you must be alive, darling. When you first started on operations you thought you were going to be taken prisoner. I pinned you down to say what you really thought and you said you would be taken prisoner, but a few months back you said you thought you would be killed. But even remembering that doesn't take away the feeling of real hope I have tonight.

I didn't sleep much last night waiting for the bangs so am going to try now. Goodnight and God bless you, beloved.

21st June   Wednesday   12.45 am   *—3s 1d*

Got up late as neither Daddy or Jean slept a wink in the shelter and they came back to bed about 5 am. They have gone down again tonight. I got to the Hungaria in time for lunch with Barbara. She had her windows blown in at the Park Lane last night. An RP came down on the balloon site in Green Park. When it happened she dashed into the corridor and met some bloke in the steel business and they talked for the rest of the night and she met him for coffee at Fortnums today! We had a long and revealing natter about Molly and her friendship with a local man. I can't remember his name but it sounds as if they are quite fond of each other.

Lloyds paid in £27 odd into Bodger today and I got all excited and hopeful as it was made out to you and not paid to me and thought the accounts department had had news of you before me, but all my hopes were dashed when I read my book of words about pay to missing officers. They had said they were sending it. Oh, well, let's hope no news is a good thing, dear heart. Goodnight now, my darling. God keep you safe for me.

22nd June   Thursday   12 am
Here I am at Andover, dearest, staying at the Black Swan. Daddy and Jean suddenly decided they must go away at once as she was in such a ghastly jitter this morning. We had a pretty bad night, the RPs brought down tiles and plaster in my room. One was so close at 4.45 this morning I thought it must have come down on Oak Hill, so I phoned Muriel at 5 am to see if she was alright. She was shaken but O.K. and the bomb was about $\frac{1}{2}$ mile away! I caught the 5.35 pm down here – slow train and rotten journey. I am too old and sad for pub life, my own. I never had such a boring evening. Thousands of Americans, and faces I had

never seen before. I was so glad when it was time to wash up. I have had about four lagers and the smoky atmosphere has given me a headache.

Had very little sleep last night, my darling, so here goes. God bless you, I adore you.

23rd June   Friday   1.15 am

Georgie darling, I feel *so* superior watching people getting pickled and the lovely part is I *really* don't want to drink except with you.

This morning we went into Andover, shopped at Harold Cordy's. He gave us butter, meat and bits and pieces and gave me back my emergency card and a basket of strawberries: the Black Swan doesn't open in the mornings at all and not until 8 at night. When we returned to the pub I arranged some flowers I had bought Mabel. We had lunch and I slept till six, when Freddie turned on the wireless. It has been absolute heaven to have so much unbroken sleep. I slept last night from the time I finished writing to you until six am without a break, which is the longest since you left me, darling. Tonight Deb, Roley, Bill, Gordon and Chris came down and stayed till just now along with Mum and Dad Maloney.

I had to keep my mind very occupied or I should have burst into tears, I wanted you so much, darling. Oh, come back to me soon, beloved, life is not worth living without you. Goodnight and God bless and keep you safe, my own.

24th June   Saturday   12.50 am

A beautiful sunny day, darling. I did the bedrooms this morning, then Mabs and I had our hair done in Andover. The water was cold so have come back with mine all sticky! Slept in the garden this afternoon. Fred did not open all day but Deb, Roley, Bill, Gordon, Vi, David and Oak and a couple called Vernieux came round for drinks about 8 pm and stayed till 11. The latter two seemed a nice young couple. He is regular RAF, knows Guy Lockhart and was at Whillon in 1942 on Stirlings. He has been pretty badly shot up and is on some sort of sick leave at the moment. She seemed an awfully nice girl and they have a little girl of three and a half. Oakie has been trying to flirt with Bill Linnit much to everyone's amusement and Bill's horror!

There is some talk of Mabs, Fred and me going to Petersfield for a couple of days and I would like to see Sal for myself. Did I tell you I have asked either Dorrie or Bertie Arnold to go into the flat every day so they can send on any mail to me and open anything from the Air Ministry and telephone me immediately? I don't feel so cut off then, in case there is any news from you, my own.

Oh, Georgie, I miss you more and more. Goodnight, and God keep you safe.

25th June   Sunday   12.30 am

Another restful day, my darling. I helped with the housework, then sat in the garden altering a slip. Harold Cordy drove a beautiful pony over here at about 12.30 and the Harker contingent arrived soon after, as well as Mr and Mrs Vernieux and her sister, who lost her husband in the Middle East this year. She was telling me that her pension for herself and little girl is £210, out of which she has to pay £36 income tax. Rather dreadful isn't it? Slept this afternoon and the Harkers came down again tonight including Chrissie. They were all very sweet and we had a lovely party. Fred gave Mabs a lovely little watch which Bill Linnit had bought in Cairo. They all left at about 11.30 and we waited up to hear the midnight news.

I have not mentioned the war news for a day or two, but we have been waiting for the fall of Cherbourg in which a few German divisions are beseiged by Americans. Tonight Germany have announced that they have lost the port, but we have not yet made any such claim. I think it must be right. The RAF have been slaughtering the Robot plane bases and have got ten today. They are still coming over in good numbers. The Russians are advancing well. In Italy the weather is holding up the proceedings. That is about all I know of interest. Mabel and Fred made no moves to go to Petersfield today and as it is so peaceful and lovely here I did not push the plan at all. Mabs is still sleeping badly and taking heaps of Neurinase. Must to sleep now, my baby. Goodnight, may God bless and keep you.

26th June   Monday   2 am

Oh Georgie, my own, I have never missed you more than tonight. I love you so and the hurt never seems to get any better. I feel I just can't bear it without you another minute.

Fred and I went into Andover to shop this morning. I caught the bus in on my own this afternoon, to view some furniture, and tonight Bill Thompson, Fred, Mabel and I walked over to Abbotts Ann. I went to see Toppy and Peter and took them over to the pub for a drink and we stayed till 1 am. David brought us back. They were all so happy, laughing and talking and it was all I could do to keep from sobbing out loud.

This morning I had a letter from a garage in Cambridge saying Mrs Dodson had said I wished to garage the car with them. It would cost 30s per month! What a beast not to have told me she was fed up with having it. Now I don't know what to do. They say it is not worth much. I don't want to sell it if you are coming back because I know how you love it. But 30s a month is a bit much, isn't it? Shall have to think it out.

Goodnight, my best beloved. Sleep well and God bless you.

27th June   Tuesday   10.15 pm

An early night, thank goodness. This morning Fred, Mabel and I went into a sale at Andover – lovely stuff but terrific prices – I bid for a Knoll settee and one Knoll chair. They fetched £42, which was too much, considering the condition they were in. It was funny to go to a sale in Andover and be greeted by dealers I have met with Daddy round London. Later I walked round to Bill's to telephone Sal. Miss Nagel says she is quite alright again now.

The pub has been closed all day and no friends in this evening, thank goodness, so I have been able to slip away early and write to my boy. I did not sleep very much last night, had a dreadful attack of miseries. The more I see of the women in this village, the more I wonder whatever sort of ideas the Americans are going to have of British women. As far as I can make out any one of them will prostitute herself for 1lb of margarine! I am horrified.

I seem to have got to the middle of the book, I pray I shall have good news of you before I get to the end, darling. Have only just noticed I started at the wrong end.

Goodnight and God bless, my own darling man.

28th June   Wednesday   12.50 am

A very wet day, dearest. This afternoon – oh before I get there – I must tell you I called at Bill's to phone Marjorie Hughes. She tells me Cecil Cohen has had a doodlebug on their place and are all at sixes and sevens for the moment so naturally he does not want to see me for a bit. Day said in her letter one dropped 50 yards from the school last week and blew a few of their windows out. They are still coming over in their thousands. Anyway, this afternoon I slept, and tonight the pub was open but quiet because of the rain.

About the war: there were four German divisions in Cherbourg when they capitulated. Our losses have been 13,000, the Americans 24,000. In Italy, since the campaign started, we have lost 70,000, the Americans 62,000. In Russia they have taken another 3,000 towns today and are forging ahead. In Normandy I think the battle will now move to Caen and round there.

There has been nothing but bad news for the Germans for the last three months. Goodnight, my own darling husband. God bless and keep you safe.

29th June   Thursday   1 am
Have had such a feeling of expectancy today, darling. I felt that something important was happening to you this morning and did so hope I might have had news. Had a sweet letter from Daddy Ridley this morning. Poor old man, he must be wandering because he said they had had news of Ray in three weeks and I know it was seven or eight.

It has been a wet and miserable day. More RPs everywhere but news on all fronts is good. The Russians have polished off 70,000 Germans since their new offensive started a week ago, and have taken 6,000 villages and towns! That is about all, I think. The French patriots have killed Henriot.

This morning I walked round to Bill's and had a lovely bath. This afternoon I was going to David to see if there were any mushrooms but it poured, so I sewed and ironed instead. A quiet evening in the pub. David was running a dance at Quarley which he wanted Bill and me to go to. No thank you, not without my Georgie.

Bill, Fred, Mabel and I played some good darts, the

first since we played in the Red Lion, darling. Toppy and Peter came over and want me to have their cottage for the kids' holidays. I don't think it is a bad idea as they will be out all day with the harvest. Should prefer something of my own but there is nothing, and I don't want to be too near this place, then I have an excuse for not coming over too often. I wonder if we shall have notice from the Roberts because of the RPs?

Goodnight and God bless you and look after you, my own beloved man.

30th June   Friday   12 am

Desperately sad without you today, my dearest. The last day of June and no news. There is nothing in life without you, my darling, I feel absolutely desperate tonight.

This morning Chris, Gordon, Mabs, Fred and I went into Andover. Sewed this afternoon and slept a little (practically no sleep last night). Tonight the pub was open for a short time. Deb and Roley came down from London full of RP reports. They had a good harvest today as they hit the Regent Palace and Bush House. It blew all the windows and papers out of offices as far away as Beak Street! Bill Linnit went to a meeting tonight and I am afraid they are going to close the theatres as it has been such a ghastly two weeks. We shall hear when he comes down tomorrow. Just what Goebbels wants of course, but as London is in flames now, according to him, he can't make much more out of it.

Letter from Jean this morning, she and Daddy are enjoying the break and she says her nerves are back to normal now.

The Germans counter-attacked in Normandy last night, the heaviest battle so far, and were beaten off in four hours. We have made more progress, and the Russians have now killed 80,000 Germans this week and are attacking Minsk. They are about 580 miles from Berlin and we 625 miles. Fred says that at the rate they are going they should be there next weekend:

Well, shall now cry myself to sleep, my Georgie. Oh I want you so. Goodnight, and may God send you home to me soon.

JULY

1st July   Saturday   12.30 am

A happy new month, my baby. I had such a lovely dream of you this morning, only the second I have had all the time you have been away. I was loving you and all the time I remember trying to tell you how lucky we were to be together even in a dream. It was latish this morning because I looked at my watch as soon as I awoke and it was 7.30.

Nothing much this morning; I sewed most of the time. Went for a walk this afternoon and finished up in Monxton Church. It's the first time I have ever been there, but I have been feeling I wanted to pray for you in church for sometime and have not made the opportunity. Have felt so close to you all day my darling, but was rather shattered in church by the hymns which were up for tomorrow. I thought they might help me, but they were all about our valiant dead.

I really must go back on Thursday. I think Daddy and Jean should be back by then and I am terribly bored with life here. Pub life is all right for a weekend but no more. David and Oak are going to let me take back two chickens and three dozen eggs so that will please Jeannie.

If only you knew how terribly incomplete life is without you, my own husband. Oh, please God, you are alive and can come back to me. Blind, no arms, no legs, anyhow, I want you for ever and ever and will love and look after you all my life. Goodnight, beloved.

2nd July   Sunday   1 am

I'm fed up with these late nights, my darling, I feel so tired and bored when I come to bed, I can't write anything of interest to you.

This morning I walked through Grately to Oak's to see if there were any mushrooms. There were not more than half a dozen. It has been muggy and raining solidly for a week. The whole country has been crying out for rain for nearly three months, and of course it has to come the week after the Invasion started. Consequently, the troops are having a bloody time, visibility is nil for the RAF, both for bombing and stopping the RPs. Wells in the villages are bone dry and they have been having to go down to the river, which is very low. Tonight the pub opened at 9 pm. Deb, Roley, Gordon and Bill Linnit stayed till 12.30 and were very amusing. But I have a rotten tummy ache tonight darling, so am going to lay me down to sleep.

May God bless you, and comfort you. Goodnight, dearest.

3rd July   Monday   11.30 pm

So sad and depressed today. Where are you, Georgie? This morning Bill Thompson and I caught the 10 am bus into Andover and then walked out to Charlton. Harold Cordy is going to bid for 100 acres of ground there called Old Downs Farm on Monday, and has promised me I can have the cottage on it if I want it, so I thought before I got too interested and committed myself I would have a quiet snoop. I don't really think it matters. It is only ten minutes from And-over Station and just above those awful little villas which lead out of Junction Road. It certainly overlooks a nice field, and is high, but I am wondering about fur-niture. It will cost rather a lot at present day prices. Would Toppy's be better for the holidays? If I start a job it is nice and near the station but that is about all to recommend it as far as I can see. I shall go with Harold to see it before I return on Thursday, I expect.

Very quiet night in the pub. When we closed Mabel, Fred and I had two games of shanghai and here I am in bed fairly early, thank goodness.

Still have not had the Queen's Gate rent for June 1st. Goodnight, and God bless and guide you, my own man.

4th July   Tuesday   11.15 pm
A fairly quiet day, dearest. Better weather, which gave our airforce a chance in Normandy while our fighters had a go at the doodlebug. I heard tonight that Daddy's shop windows are out and also something about Stodge and Muriel, but I couldn't make out if it was in Surbiton or London. Just as well I am going back on Thursday in case the old boy is in a flap. I can't think how they shut up shop at night! This morning I sewed, and cooked the lunch. This

afternoon Bill and I went to the pictures. Back to hers for tea at 6.30 pm. Pub opened for an hour tonight. I stewed some mushrooms which we had when the pub was shut.

Georgie, my own, I am beginning to get terribly despondent, darling. It will be ten weeks on Friday. Oh, my darling, I *can't* go on without you. There is nothing in life that means a thing. I look at the different people who come into the pub and compare them with you and all our friends in the Squadron and they make me sick. I can't be civil to anyone because I begrudge them being here when you are not. Mabel and Fred have been awfully good and kind to me and I enjoyed the change for the first week, but now it is getting irksome. I am alright when things are fresh and distract my thoughts, but as soon as I get used to it I want to move on.

The reason I write about how I feel and what I think all the time, darling, is because I dare not let myself think what you are feeling. Can you understand that, I wonder. Goodnight – God bless you, beloved.

5th July   Wednesday   12.30 am
This morning I walked to Abbotts Ann to see if I could sort things out with Tops about the cottage and wish Peter many happy returns as it is his birthday today. I arrived about 10.20 and they were out. Started to walk into Andover and fortunately met them on the way. Peter ran me into the sale at the Starter where I was to meet Mabel and Fred. Slept this afternoon.

I have not quite decided which train to catch tomorrow as I could not get through to the station to find out whether the 12.26 stops at Surbiton.

Had a letter from Daddy this morning to say all the windows are out of the emporium but he still intends to stay away another couple of weeks and is looking for some fishing! Weather bad again today so our advances are not terrific. The Russians have taken Minsk. Afraid my pencil is very faint, but every night since I have been here I have been writing by torch light. A fortress crashed on a café in the Salisbury Road today and made a nasty mess. Won't go into details, they worried me too much. Goodnight, my own darling husband. God bring you back to me soon or else let me join you.

6th July   Thursday   8.30 pm   Surbiton

Back to Surbiton, my darling. Couldn't stand pub life another second, sweet as they have all been to me. I caught a slow train because it was supposed to stop at Surbiton – of course it didn't! So I had to change at Woking complete with two suitcases, six dozen eggs, two chickens and your dispatch case in which, I think I have told you, I keep this book and never let it leave my side. A porter at Surbiton said he would deliver the cases, but didn't get them until just now. The old fool had delivered them to Glenbuck Court! The doodle-bugs got the County Hall on the road to Kingston last night, apparently.

Churchill made his first public speech on flying bombs today. We have had 2,754 and they have killed

2,752 people and injured 8,000. He says London would have got them six months ago if it had not been for the bombing. According to the news 2,000 planes attacked the bomb bases today, so that may account for the fact that there has not been a siren since I have been back.

Shall go to town tomorrow, all being well, and take one of the chickens to Marjorie Hughes and some eggs to Rosie. Have just fallen down these blasted stairs and cut my knees *and*, worse, torn my stockings.

I phoned Judy Lockhart tonight to see if she had heard anything and perhaps been trying to get in touch with me. She was at the American Red Cross but I spoke to her sister; they still know nothing. Did I tell you that evacuation of women and children is in full swing again?

50,000 tons of bombs have been dropped on the RP bases. Deep shelters by the tube entrances are being opened, there are eight of them, four north of the river and four south, and they each have 8,000 bunks. These dormitories are divided into sections to give each family privacy. They have restaurants, sick bays, modern sanitation and all are 100 feet below ground.

Today has been a beautiful day (just because I have left the country). Bill Thompson has insisted that I go to her if I get frightened here by myself. I had to come back though, to see if Marjorie is keeping in touch with Cecil Cohen and if Don has any big objection to me taking the children to Abbotts Ann. I can't find anywhere else, so he will have to lump it, I think. It is going to be heaven to have a bath and go to bed early. I do hope it is not going to be a noisy night. Mr Wardle says I am mad to sleep up here by myself and I should go down to the Arnolds. I think I will see what it is like tonight first. Going to bed now, my beloved. Good-night, and God bless you and comfort you and give you patience and confidence in me, because I know you will be worrying, my poor darling.

7th July   Friday   9.30 pm

It is grand being able to write to you with a table to lean on, darling. It was quite a quiet night I think. I heard the siren about midnight and the all clear at seven. Don't know what dropped in between times! The sirens have been wailing all day long today. I got up about eight, did some ironing and then went up to Cecilia's. Harold Cordy had not taken my coupons out of the ration book so I got two weeks' supplies from them! I caught a train about 11.45 to town. Had lunch in the office with the girls. Saw Carol and suggested the Abbotts Ann idea and she seemed delighted. Evidently they had not thought of anything. Stodge wants to bring little John down for August Bank Holiday week. So have written to Toppy asking her to get a room for that week near the cottage if possible. Took the eggs to Rosie. Marjorie not there so gave the chicken to Miss C (can't remember her name – perfumery at Derry's: this happens such a lot since you have been away). Her sister is very ill so she was delighted with it. Apparently her sister had to be evacuated from St George's Hospital as the barracks at Chelsea were hit and so many of the

97

soldiers were taken to St George's . . . . slight
diversion while I run to window to watch Doodlebug
drop. It came straight across the Gables and dropped
in Kingston. Perfect view from my bedroom window!
Bloody things.

Had an annoying journey back from Kensington to
Waterloo as the tube was closed after Charing Cross
and had to get an emergency bus. Home about 4.30,
tea. Needlework and read till 8 pm. Had a chop and
some peas, have just washed up and am now going to
have a bath and go to bed. Do hope I shall be able to
sleep as well as I did last night. I had a tiny dream about
you. I was at the top of a large tall building, watching
some people coming across the road and I suddenly saw
you. I was so excited I didn't wait for the lift but dashed
down the stairs; of course you had caught the lift up
before I could reach you, so I ran all the way up the
stairs and there you were, my beloved. You took me
out and insisted on buying me a pair of evening shoes,
quite useless ones, black and lamé! But it was heaven
to be with you for a few minutes, if only in a dream.

I am so *terribly terribly* lonely and unhappy —— now
I've blotched another page by crying all over it. There
will be a good few you won't be able to read if you ever
come back to me. I am losing hope, Georgie – what
shall I do? Goodnight my darling, God bless you.

8th July   Saturday   11 pm

Writing in bed, darling, I'm so tired. The flat has
been bombed! It happened last Wednesday at 5 pm.

The Secretarial College and house next to it had a direct hit.

Our flat is complete and utter chaos. The Roberts are away and no one had notified them or us. I phoned Harrods this morning asking why the June rent had not been paid and he told me about this bomb and advised me to go and have a look. The roof is nearly all in. All windows and doors have blown out and most of the ceilings are down. It is knee deep in glass, plaster and soot. The furniture has come off fairly well except for your lovely bureau which is pockmarked all over. Nelly, bless her, has been there cleaning all day and every day since Wednesday and has performed wonders.

Funnily enough, I found we were not insured against war damage and did it yesterday – of course too late! Anyway, having walked all over Kensington from one place to another I have collected a bundle of forms to fill in, and find the government compensate you and me and the two kids to the extent of £350. That will easily cover all the cleaning, recovering of chairs and French polishing necessary I think, so we are lucky in that way and I will leave the new insurance in, in case it happens again. I have to get someone there to estimate the damage and put in a claim. If I have to move the stuff (and I don't know how long the menders take with the windows and roof), Chris has lent me their barn which will save the cost of storing. On the other hand I am going to miss that steady income of £6 6s od clear profit per week, aren't I? So should I try and get another flat when I have had the thing cleaned? The

Civil Defence people advised me, very wisely I think, to put in my claim but not to have anything done till the furniture comes out of storage. The Roberts have not come to help me. All he said was, 'Oh, I'll send someone for my clothes tomorrow. (They are in Norfolk). The Harding Finlaysons and McCluskys were charming, their flats are pretty bad but the Moyles and Humphrey Owens were hardly touched except for broken glass. Ours is the worst and of course if it rains before anything is done it is going to ruin everything. I moved everything I could away from the windows and stacked it under the inside walls, but I could not get up the carpets to turn them back, they are too well tacked.

My brain is in a whirl trying to think out what to do. Mr Woodard at Harrods went on holiday today which may be a good thing as the manager has taken it over. He is a Mr Umpleby who I think came to our house in Surbiton when I was a little girl and his father did business with Daddy, so that may be a help. The lift shaft is shattered to bits. When I opened the dining-room door I wondered if the soda cylinder had blown up, but it hadn't and that ceiling is not down, but everything is covered in broken glass.

I must try and go to sleep now, dear heart. Goodnight and God bless you, darling.

9th July   Sunday   9.30 pm
Dorrie, Bertie and I caught the 9 am train up to Queen's Gate this morning. He says all the furniture

can easily be restored and we are very lucky, really. Nelly was there working when we arrived. I took her some eggs and gave her £1 for the work she was doing for me. She is not supposed to work there on Sundays.

I saw the Light Rescue people about carting away the plaster, glass and rubble. Naturally the lift shaft has collapsed and it is impossible for Nelly to carry all that lot down. It rained last night, worst luck, and has ruined the mattress in the spare room. It was a lousy one anyway! Otherwise it has not come in much. It does not come through the windows but through the roof and where the ceilings are down.

Shall see Harrods tomorrow about the situation concerning Roberts' rent, etc.

I talked with the war damage man today and he says they will have the place watertight by Tuesday, but that they will not put up the ceilings till the RPs stop. As Churchill says, it may be some months and we also have the rocket bomb to look forward to, so it does not look as if the Roberts would be able to go back there. If Harrods say there is no demand for flats I shall definitely take the furniture to Monxton. Perhaps I can furnish a cottage there and let it to make a little money.

We got back to lunch. Bertie went on duty and Dorrie came up to me. We had eggs for tea and then went to the pictures. Just back, I have washed my hair and here I am writing to you. I am so thankful our beautiful picture is O.K., darling.

Now about finance: as you know I have been paying

my allowance into Bodger. Now I shall have to live on that and we shall only be able to save Green Hearn's allowance. Must phone him tomorrow and tell him to only buy £10 saving certs every month, stop rent and pay Barkers £7 17s 6d as usual. Everything else is finished. I often wonder if Cyril will come down on me for the money I think we must still owe him.

When I phoned Colin about insurance last night he was telling me about a friend of his who was adrift on the Continent and without being able to speak German or French, spent Christmas in a Brussels hotel! I can hardly believe that. Who would they think he was – aren't the Germans at war with all the English speaking nations? Must drop the kids a line and let them know they are going to Abbots Ann for their holidays. Sandler is playing his usual Sunday Palm Court stuff and making me feel very sad. Goodnight, my darling. May God guide you and bring you safely home to me.

10th July   Monday   9 pm

Such a busy day at the flat – or what is left of it. I saw Harrods and they say it is a waste of time to take an inventory. They charge three guineas and we wouldn't know if anything damaged was caused by Roberts or the bombing. Then I phoned Deb and she put me on to someone who will move the furniture. You are not allowed to take it by road over 50 miles, so I was lucky to fix up with a little man for about £12 10s od. She also gave me the name of cleaners where I can take all the carpets, curtains, bedding etc.

I threw in quite a lot of your suits as the lid of the coffin was opened and they got sprayed with glass and soot. They are being collected tomorrow.

Harrods will take nothing for three months and no one will store things, so I have been very lucky. I had lunch with Stodge at a new place next to Claridges called Sherry's. Not bad for 5s, no cover charge.

Then back to the flat to try and sort out the stuff in the dining room. I think it would be quite a good idea for me to lend Gordon our syphon thing as they are letting us have the barn, don't you? Have a lot of the bottles here, as we had them at Cambridge. I'll take them up with me tomorrow, then everything can go at once.

Caught a train home about 6.30 pm and here I am. Don't enjoy working up in the flat while the Doodles are going over, bits more ceiling keep dropping and you never know if the rest of the roof will cave in. Think I will cook myself some bacon and an egg and then to bed.

Goodnight my darling, God bless you.

11th July   Tuesday   11 pm   *+4s 6d*

To the flat this morning darling, and what do you think – another damn Doodlebug fell outside the Museum and brought down the rest of our ceilings. Nelly was so nervy and fed up that all her work of clearing up was undone that she cried and nearly fainted. I gave her some of the Roberts' whisky and had a tiny drop myself. It really was medicinal darling, I was so shaky. Anyway there was no more glass to fall and the mirrors are still all right. I was to have met Deb for lunch but I was so dirty and my hair so full of plaster I put it off.

The cleaners did not turn up for the things while I was there. Before anything I went round to the District Valuers office to make sure it is in order to move the furniture, etc. at once and they said perfectly all right. I have written to Mr Allen today thanking him for letting us have the flat. I phoned Bodger this morning and stopped the rent, so hope that is all in order and he won't want a month's rent; Harrods did not seem to think I could get it from the Roberts. Mrs Shuter phoned tonight to say how sorry she was that I had had another blow, also Judy Lockhart. She was miserable, and upset me by saying she had given up hope because she could not possibly see how eight men could disappear for ten and a half weeks. If we had heard of one of the crew she thinks there might be a chance. Of course the Germans are slowing up on giving out news of prisoners. Oh, my dearest, I can't give up hope, you must come back to me.

Dorrie and Bertie came up this evening to play solo. It is company while the sirens are wailing on and off. I think we had seven between 7.30 and 10.30!

Goodnight, beloved. God bless you.

12th July   Wednesday   10.15
Another busy day at the flat. The most difficult thing to get sorted out is our dining room full of junk!

Having got everything arranged for the men to move the stuff on Friday, the man phoned at 10 o'clock tonight to say he can do it tomorrow. All I hope is that he can disconnect the gas cooker as I don't expect the gasman till Friday morning.

Have just phoned Gordon and told him the stuff will be there tomorrow and that I am sending the soda water machine and bottles for them to use. It will help pay them back a little for their kindness.

A letter from Hugh was waiting when I got back this afternoon. He seems quite well but terribly upset about you. Is keeping his fingers crossed.

Mrs Roberts phoned to say he is not well but she will be up tomorrow; glad she is going to be here before I take everything away. Shall have to go to the bank and get some money to give these moving men. I suppose ten per cent again. They are charging £12 for the job which is really ridiculously cheap. I wonder if I can claim that from the insurance? Must go to bed, my own, or I shall have to do the blackout in the lounge where I am writing this. It is a joy to be on my own, where I can bring this book out and write on a table.

Goodnight, beloved. God bless and keep you. I love you so terribly.

13th July   Thursday   8.20 pm

Well, darling, that is the end of our lovely flat. The men came at 10 am and finished loading at 4 pm. They will not deliver the things to Monxton till 10 am tomorrow morning. Have just phoned Chris to tell her the time and that the soda water machine was coming and she tells me they have one! What a pity.

Mrs Roberts arrived at midday. She agreed the damages with me and I tried to get her to settle for three bottles of gin, one whisky and one Kummel which were in the sideboard, but she wouldn't play, so have bunged the list into Harrods and I hope it costs them more! (Don't think it will.) Anyway she was very good to Nellie. Gave her £5 over her wages. I gave her £2, so she is cock-a-hoop and says she will work for me if I come back to London any time!

I gave the men 30s, hope it was enough. There were three of them and the foreman seemed very satisfied. Am terribly tired now. Dear old Nellie; there was half a bottle of gin left which Mrs Roberts had given her, and she insisted upon me having it. I pinched a bottle of whisky, so that makes something towards a party, dearest, when you get back.

The Russians are only 25 miles away from East Prussia: Germans must be feeling a bit shaky. Last night was wonderful, no alert for the first time for 27 days when the Doodles started.

It is pouring with rain again today, so I am really glad to have got the things away. Rain was pouring in through the roof, running all down the lounge walls and across the floors. I think I have done everything with regards to telephone, gas, electricity, etc. Have asked for deposits back, but they will subtract them from the Roberts' bill, and make a mess of that I expect.

So tired darling, am going to bed now. Must devote

some time to *this* flat tomorrow. Goodnight, my own darling husband, may God comfort you and bring you safely home to me.

14th July   Friday   11 pm   +2s 3d

A nice quiet day darling, after the rush of bombs and moving, etc. Plenty of alerts but nothing seemed very near. I stayed in bed till 9 am, then had a good clear up in the flat and went out shopping. Dorrie and I went to a film this afternoon and saw *Princess O'Rorke* – quite amusing and nothing to do with the war for a change. Tonight they came up and played solo.

Westley has sent eight bottles of gin, two rums and four and a half whiskies. So they will be kept till your return. Whisky is more and more difficult to get hold of.

I keep on wondering whether it is good or bad that it is eleven weeks today without a word from you, my own; not only you but all the crew. Surely, unless the aircraft was blown up in mid air that must be a *good* sign. I remember you have always said good news usually takes longer. Please God it is so in our case. Tomorrow I am lunching with Judy Lockhart and not looking forward to it – she is so pessimistic now and talks such a lot.

The estimate for our cleaning came in today, £47 13s 6d. Not bad I think. The big lounge carpet was only £6 odd.

Goodnight my darling, God bless you. I have confidence in your safety tonight.

15th July   Saturday   11 pm
St Swithin's day – a little rain.

I had arranged to meet Judy Lockhart at the Hungaria at 12.30 (her suggestion), but she arrived at 1.10. Cost me a small fortune in tomato juice!

She arrived wearing a tweed suit with her hair all wet as there had been quite a heavy shower. She said she couldn't get a taxi and had to walk miles which, I suppose, was why she was so late! It was even worse than I had expected, she is most pessimistic about the crew's chances.

I saw Marjorie Hughes today. She was charming and I told her I would like to see Cecil Cohen before I go away, so shall try and make an appointment to see him on Monday.

I had a very nice letter from Mrs Allen offering me the basement flat in Queen's Gate when it has been done up. So I phoned Mrs McClusky to find out what it consisted of. I had only been in one lovely large room. She said there were two very large rooms, beautifully tiled bathroom and kitchenette and she thought the rent was about £100. With constant hot water and a good address that is pretty cheap. She says the sun pours into both rooms, not like some basements. It might do for me for work and for us both as a kicking off place after the war. Goodnight, and God bless you my beloved, I am sure He is taking care of you somewhere. I pray for miracles for you.

16th July   Sunday   11.10 pm

A very quiet day, darling. I washed, ironed, sewed and read until 5 pm. Then Dorrie and Bertie asked me to go down to them for tea. While I was there Bertie made out the estimate for the furniture from the Queen's Gate flat to be repolished, repaired, etc. It comes to £108 odd. I don't expect the War Damage people will pay the full amount. Altogether it will be about £160. So I expect we shall get about £125 don't you?

Tomorrow I am going to have a look at that downstairs flat at Queen's Gate. I don't think I shall get anything much cheaper than that, do you?

Today a telegraph boy on a motorbike came dashing into the garden. I got all het up, but he went into the next block.

I have sorted out all my papers today. I put all the important ones in your dispatch case with this book and I have written stacks of letters, including one to Group Captain Coombes. I want to make absolutely certain nothing has been heard of any of your crew, my beloved, and to hear all the Squadron news. On Tuesday I shall go across to the shop to open it up and see if I can do any business. Don't expect so as there are no windows! Can't remember if I told you they had been boarded up. The old man is apparently not returning till August 4th.

Two Doodles fell smack in the middle of the line at Malden and Wimbledon today, and do you know the Railway men had got all the lines O.K. and trains running by 6 pm tonight. It happened at lunch time and wrecked every line in both places. Pretty good of them, I thought.

I am full of hope, my adored man. I think you will come home to me one day. God bless you and keep you safe till then.

17th July   Monday   9.15 pm

Quite a satisfactory day, my dearest. I phoned Cecil Cohen this morning and he said go and see him right away. He seemed a very nice straightforward Jew. His idea is to open a showroom for a subsidiary company called 'Mademoiselle' as soon as the Doodles have stopped. I think he likes me and I should like to run the company for him; being a young firm I could make so much of it. Anyway there is absolutely nothing doing while the bombs are still pouring down on London. I thought I would ask Lionel about it (and him) because I know you trust Lionel and I felt he would tell me the truth. He says Cohen is a grand chap, absolutely trustworthy and that it is an old established firm. The trouble is going to be how long the bombing continues. When one looks at a map of Europe, our little bit of Normandy looks horribly small and it seems as if we shall be quite a time taking the part of the coast where they send the buggers from.

It has been a beautiful day today – the first for weeks. Unfortunately it was heralded by a very heavy mist this morning and the Doodles started dropping all round Surbiton about 5 am. The Lancs are bombing by day, going in formation with fighter cover. If we have some decent weather we should make some headway at last. Unfortunately it was heralded by a very heavy mist this morning and the doodles started dropping all round Surbiton about 5 am. The Lancs are bombing by day, going in formation with fighter cover. If we have some decent weather we should make some headway at last.

Lionel was so sweet when I saw him today. He was upset about the flat and asked if I needed any money! Gave me a new book by Somerset Maugham. I will take him some eggs tomorrow. I saw Kelsall who told me he was taken prisoner in the last war and his people did not hear of him for three months. Dear little man gave me £28 18s. It will pay for the move anyway.

Did I tell you Dorrie has got the sack as she stayed away a month and old Evans has had *all* his shops bombed and bombed again? They are being very kind to me while I am here on my own and when the Doodles drop I dash down to them for cover. Am going to bed to read my new book.

Goodnight, my own darling and only man. May God bring you home soon.

18th July   Tuesday   —*8s*

Quiet day at Surbiton and fetched my lovely petit point seat covers from the cleaners. They have come up very well. This afternoon Dorrie came to Kingston with me. I want to give Mabel a fruit set and a small swing mirror. We tramped around every shop but could not get either. A very noisy day with the doodlebugs.

I have bought a bicycle for £8. It is a brand new Hercules but wartime make, it has black handle bars instead of chromium which I hate, but the tyres are new which is something, and it will be fun with the kids. I have written to Mabs to ask if I can go down this weekend and stay there before I go over to Toppy's. I am getting a bit nervy again. One keeps listening for these blasted things all day long. No news today, my own. Goodnight, God bless you and keep you safe.

19th July   Wednesday

Went up to town darling, and took Lionel the eggs I promised him.

Had lunch in the office with Stodge and Muriel and then spent the whole afternoon, till 6 pm, trying to cope with the Assistance Board. I really do not see why I should fork out nearly £50 for cleaning. They took thousands of particulars, filled in dozens of forms and have now referred me to Winchester, which is apparently the nearest place to where I am going to stay in Abbotts Ann! I was very relieved to hear that they will pay the whole claim which, with the estimate for mending furniture, comes to £157 – in a few months. I thought it would be after the war!

Stodge and John (little) are coming down on September 8th, she for the two weekends, he to stay the week with me and the girls. I did not sleep more than an hour last night, Doodles came over in their hundreds, all going towards London. Several landed in the poor old City again.

News is good on all fronts, terrific bombing in Normandy and an advance today in consequence! Also advances in Italy and Russia.

Montgomery says we have accounted for thousands of Germans in Normandy. Do you remember that tough ex-sailor, Jim, at Abbotts Ann pub? There was a huge photo of him in the *Daily Mail* today. He has been blockade busting with the Merchant Navy to good purpose.

I am going to lunch at the Junior Carlton with Hal Lawson tomorrow. I know you won't mind. I accepted because he is the only person I know at the Air Ministry who may be able to give me a few details of your last op. Shall rush up and back again, as I must tidy up the flat and iron my collars and cuffs, etc.

Come home to me soon, baby mine. God bless you my beloved. I adore you more and more and more.

20th July   Thursday

Early this morning I went to Stodge's flat to collect some clothes for the kids and some stores. Then I went to the food office; as soon as I returned Stodge phoned to say Mr Selby had a proposition to put to me. So I called in there before meeting Hal Lawson. He has had a company offered to him at £3,000 with a £3,000 loss in 1940 (very good stock of 16,000 yards of woollen material which means a float of about 64,000 coupons). Would I work it for him and he wants 50 per cent of the profits. I think he also wants me to buy 50 per cent of the company. Oh yes! I went to old man Shuter to chew it over and he said it would be barmy, that Cecil Cohen's proposition is much better altogether.

I then lunched with Hal Lawson. He had phoned somebody yesterday who confirmed that absolutely nothing was known about you and your crew. Actually he was a little bit pessimistic, darling, but did suggest you might be fighting with the Maquis. If that were so I feel sure Guy (if he is alive) would have made contact with *somebody*. Hal is a Wing Commander. He told me Don Bennett had called a few days ago and he is, of course, incredibly busy right now. Actually I can imagine that being so. He also told me that Chris's wife is a great friend of his, she is such a sweetie. *Do make it back, Georgie boy. I know you will.* You always said give me a year Pip, darling. Sweetheart I'll give you 30 years if I have them to give.

Am catching the 9.17 am train to Andover tomorrow. Goodnight, and God bless and guide you, my own darling boy.

21st July Friday 11.15 pm Andover

Wonderful news this morning, darling. Generals of the German army have revolted against Hitler and yesterday they tried to kill him. The bomb was only six feet away and he escaped with burns and concussion! Just as well. He will live to be frightened another day. Such a quick get out would have been too good for him. The General who planted the bomb has been executed. Himmler is in complete command of the Army, the only orders to be obeyed are ones he issues. Same applies to Doenitz for the Navy and Goering for the Luftwaffe!

We had an awful Doodlebug night. I went down to Dorrie. Bertie was due in at six this morning but did not arrive till nearly eight. He had been digging people out from bombed buildings near Kingston Barracks. My train was late owing to the line at Clapham being hit. Fred met me. I was so tired I went to sleep waiting for my lunch! Slept all afternoon. Cellar crowded tonight, lots of old faces. I do miss you dreadfully when I am down here darling, it seems to hurt more than ever.

This business in Germany must mean that the internal unrest is much greater than we have been allowed to believe. I really feel it must hurry the end of the war. Am going to sleep now darling, without having one ear cocked for Doodles – what heaven.

Goodnight my own husband. God bless and keep you.

22nd July   Saturday   12.30 am
This morning Fred took me into Andover and I collected my bike which had been left at the station (Oak brought the rest of my luggage back in the trailer). And I cycled back to Monxton! Quite amusing as I had two flat tyres and no pump so I wandered round the outside of the station borrowing a pump from any bike that was waiting. First a girl came up and was moving off with her bike and I had to shout to her to wait as I had her pump and hoped she didn't mind. Then the same thing happened with a small boy! Eventually I mounted and

swept away. It goes very easily but the saddle is much too low and it makes my legs ache!

Fred and I played crib tonight until the pub opened at 8.30 pm. Then the Harker family arrived in cracking form. Gordon has never been funnier: they stayed until just now, so I am full up with Goldens and never want to see another! I gave Chris my little Ronson lighter. She is so good to me and she never has one. It is Mabel's birthday tomorrow, and I have kept the little Chippendale mirror I bought for her last week to give her (I feel sure I told you about walking the length of Church Street for it). Life down here without you, my baby, is absolutely hell. Please come home to me soon, Georgie boy, I love you so much. I am rude to other men who are only trying to be nice to me or even just trying to talk to me.

Goodnight my own beloved. God bless you, I adore you.

23rd July   Sunday   12.25 am

I cycled to Abbotts Ann this morning. Bike is going beautifully now Fred has raised the saddle. Can't think how Dorrie ever rode it – her legs are much longer than mine. Saw Toppy when I got there and told her I should be going over on Wednesday. She is frightfully excited about having us: they both are. She has made Day a dressing table stool, Peter is trying to borrow a horse for Sally and they really can't do enough for us.

I told you it is Mab's birthday. She was delighted with the mirror. This lunch time that Squadron Leader

Vernieux and his wife Daphne came over. They are a grand couple, you would like them very much. He is in Leicester and flew a Tiger Moth down to Andover. I was telling her all the news and happened to mention that Chris Martin is missing. Apparently they were together some place. As regards the war, the Russians are making their usual stupendous advances and taking the usual thousands of places and only half a dozen prisoners, which always amuses me. We seem to be held up a bit in Normandy by bad weather. Troops in Italy are in Pisa and the tower is still leaning! As for the internal unrest in Germany, they have clamped down everywhere and no news is coming out of the country at all. There is no doubt that it is pretty serious though. Am going to sleep now, my dearest. God bless and keep you: I adore you.

24th July   Monday   11.30 pm

A very dull day. Early this morning I called on a Mrs Granville at Chalk Pit Cottage (the one up the watery little lane) and asked her if she would like to let me the big room she has (looks like a whitewashed and thatched barn). It is fitted with electric light, a large brick fireplace and a raised platform at one end which would make a good bedroom. I thought if I take the basement flat at Queen's Gate, this would be a country retreat for weekends and very cheap. Thought I would offer her 30s per month including electricity. Water we could get from the bottom of Chris's paddock which is just across the lane. When you come back my darling, we shall not be able to afford a lot of rents and you would hate every weekend in a basement flat! This room could be made very attractive. At the moment she has chickens and ducks in there – not to mention a couple of swallows nests! I told her it would not be for two months so she is letting me know. Her people want to get away from the Doodles and she does not like to let it go at the moment.

This afternoon I went to the cinema by myself. Everyone else wanted to sleep. As I hadn't got you, I was not interested! I forgot to tell you I saw our furniture in the barn this morning. It is beautifully stacked but it is quite impossible to get anything. Chris lent me a dust sheet to cover the picture with.

Fred opened for this evening, but no crowd. Tomorrow we are going to Salisbury.

Goodnight, my darling. God bless and help you.

25th July   Tuesday   12 am
So miserable without you today, darling. Oh, Georgie boy, I don't think you are coming back to me. It will be 13 weeks on Friday and that is our lucky number. Please God it will work this time.

This morning I tried to phone Mrs Robley Browne from Bill's house. There was two hours delay so had to ask Bill to give a message. Day is supposed to be staying with the Roberts at Sunningdale and I said I must have a letter from Robley Browne first. As I have not heard from Day or her this week I am slightly anxious.

We went to Salisbury today. Pretty boring. On our

return I called at Bills to find she had gone to Newbury for the evening. So I still don't know about Day, but presume it must be alright or Bill would surely have left a message. I had a letter from Kate today, very het up with this awful waiting for news. Goodnight, God bless you and guard you my dearest; I adore you.

26th July   Wednesday   11.10 pm   Abbotts Ann
  The most ghastly thing has happened, my darling. A wire came from Robley Browne saying 'Day cannot go Roberts. Must see you here urgently. Phone me tonight. She is quite well.' I was still at Monxton, so dashed up to Chris and phoned and Mrs RB says she has been 'doing wrong'. So I said what, and she said she has been telling the other girls about sex. I don't know what on earth is going on, but Mrs RB is furious. I am worried to death and am going there tomorrow on the 7.21 am from Andover. Please God she is not going to expel her. She will never live it down with the family. I have not told a soul except Chris who I know will not tell anyone. This is the third awful thing to happen. Let's hope our luck will change now.
  I came over here tonight before supper and Peter brought my cases over this morning, so now I shall have to start housekeeping in earnest. Must go to sleep, my dearest, as I have to get up at 6.30 am. I am worried to death, darling, feel quite sick and ill.

27th July   Thursday   10.30 pm
  A terrible day, dearest. I left Andover at 7.21 am and

arrived at Hampden House at 12.30. Mrs Robley Browne was very charming but says there is no doubt Day has told two girls in her bedroom all about lesbianism. Half the school seems to know about it and she can't keep her. She apparently was told by a girl who left last term. Isn't it too ghastly? Mrs RB thinks she should be at home with me and go to a day school. Goodness knows how I shall manage, but I cannot go to town until the Doodles stop she cannot start school until then. Oh, Georgie, I am so miserable, I did not sleep a wink last night. I do so wish you were here to help me through this. The great difficulty is going to be keeping it from Don and the family. Mrs RB has agreed to say anything that will help Day, because she also agrees that it would be dreadful for her if anyone found out.

Had a letter tonight from Group Captain Combes. He is not hopeful about you now darling, after three months. Please dear God they are all wrong. I think if anything else happens I shall not be able to stand it. If I was sure you were dead I would try and come to you.

Tomorrow I pick up Sally. I have had a talk with Day and told her I will try and do all I can for her, but she must not let Sally know or say anything about the whole business ever again. Wouldn't it be dreadful if she did tell Sally? Oh I feel so sick about it all.

Goodnight my own and God bless you. I forgot to tell you we caught the 5 pm train back from Waterloo. Doodles overhead twice while we were at the station.

28th July Friday 11.5 pm

I went to Winchester on the 9.55 am bus this morning
and met Sally on the bypass as that was as far as Cress-
well could bring her. I had to take a taxi out there –
had a very good chauffeuse, and as I was not sure of
the place where I had to meet Sal she was most patient
and clever in finding her. I took Sally to lunch at the
Royal Hotel which was excellent and then back to Andover on the 3.10 bus. Day had been to the pictures with
Auntie Toppy. She seems to get over things much too
quickly. She is laughing and talking away today as if
nothing whatever was the matter. I am so terribly
worried about her, if only you were here to help me,
darling.

Toppy and Peter have not started their threshing yet.
I rather wish they would so that I can have a go at the
kitchen which is so dirty. I really don't feel I want the
food that is cooked there. A letter came from Harrods
today saying that they had at last received £38 for the
June rent, £9 6s od for the few days in July and had sent
in a bill for damages for £4 5s od.

Sally brought a six week old kitten home with her!
Thank goodness it was not mice this time. It is a miserable starved looking thing. Tops does not seem to mind
though.

Have been altering Day's frocks tonight. Goodnight,
my own dearest darling. Please God will bring you back
to me.

29th July   Saturday   10.55 pm

A very quiet day, my darling. A letter from Daddy this morning enclosing one from Hugh saying that Hermione had presented him with a nine-and-a-half pound son on June 22nd and they have called him Roger Douglas Granville Martin. Rather a mouthful isn't it? He asked Daddy to write to Hermione and the old man is not keen until the divorce goes through, which is quite understandable, but I shall try and persuade him to I think. It would be rotten if Hugh was bumped off and Daddy had not ackowledged her, wouldn't it.

I am so sad tonight, dearest. Missing you more and more every day and hope is getting less and less. This morning the kids and I caught the 10 am bus to Andover, called on Harold for the meat and returned to Monxton. We got the kids' bikes pumped up, and the jam and stores from the barn, and Peter drove me home.

A quiet evening with the kids playing rummy.

Sally came back with her hair very long and I cut it myself as I could not get it done in Andover. I cut it nice and short and it gave her such a shock when she saw it she burst into tears! I do wish T & P would start threshing. I want to clean the kitchen out, it is simply filthy.

The cleaning woman here heard her husband has been killed in Normandy today. Surprise everyone and make me the happiest woman in the world, my darling, by turning up soon. Goodnight and God keep you safe for me.

30th July   Sunday   10.20 pm

Thinking of you so much today, my dearest. I always am really but you have seemed particularly near me.

This morning the kids picked about three pounds of mushrooms which we had for breakfast.

I am trying to fatten up a beastly little kitten Sally brought back from school with her. (Can't remember if I told you – I was so thankful it was not mice.) The thing is all ribs and neck, only six weeks' old but seems to know everything, rather like a child of old parents! Nothing round, fat and cuddly about it at all.

Oh, how I wish I knew for certain that you are alive, my darling. I lie in bed and try and will your spirit to come to me; sometimes I think I can feel you near, then I think it is only because my thoughts are so concentrated on you all the time. I have your picture always by my bed and it makes me cry every time I look at it.

There is a report in the papers that Rommel was mortally hurt if not killed in a raid. He has been running the Normandy campaign which marches slowly. Russians are not far from Warsaw now! More and more rumours are creeping through of the unrest in Germany, especially in the army. Let's hope and pray they will crack soon. Goodnight my beloved, God bless you.

31st July   Monday   10.35 pm

So tired my poppet, have cycled miles! This morning I had a wonderful time cleaning out the kitchen. Toppy was very sweet about it and let me turn it out and do exactly what I wanted and it all smells a lot sweeter, believe me!

This afternoon I was in the middle of washing Sally's hair when a Captain Kitching called to see if Day had picked the mushrooms she had promised him at lunch time yesterday. We had not been out so he was unlucky. After I had washed all three heads, Sally helped Peter with his painting. He has hired a sprayer for the tackle! Day and I went mushrooming as I had promised some to Mabel. We picked about four pounds and did my back ache. It is uphill all the way for cycling and then all that bending! We had supper and then cycled over to the Duck to give the mushrooms to Mabel.

I had a cheque from Harrods today for the June rent, the rest to follow presumably. It has been a lovely hot summer day, starting off with a terrific mist this morning and I feel really burned and sleepy.

Goodnight, and God bless you my darling.

AUGUST

1st August   Tuesday   11.30 pm

A happy (?) new month, my own. Personally I never felt more miserable.

This morning we cycled to Brocks for some eggs. Its a long ride from here. Called at the Duck on the way back. This afternoon the children spent haymaking at Whatley's (the milkman) and had a wonderful time. They were not home until nearly 8 pm. There was a wire from Don asking me to ring him at 8. I did, and he and Carol are coming down tomorrow for the night. I have thought and thought and think I must tell him about Day for it to make sense about her leaving school. I do wish Carol was not coming though. I have taken a room for them with our cleaning woman. Do so long for you to be here to back me up, my darling. It is going to be ghastly without you. Goodnight, and God keep and help you, my beloved.

2nd August   Wednesday   10.55 pm

My beloved, thank goodness they did not come. A wire arrived at 7.20 while we were waiting for dinner to say that Don could not get away, will I go up tomorrow early. Blasted nuisance, but am so relieved they did not turn up.

This morning I went into Andover and got a beautiful

piece of steak from Harold. Peter went to Trilby and got about nine pounds of beef! This afternoon the kids went to look for mushrooms and we had a lovely meal ready. We have put the kids in the caravan and made up their bed for Don and Carol. They were so thrilled with the idea I have let them stay there even though D and C aren't coming now.

Tonight Toppy and I went over to the Duck for an hour – we bicycled. She used Day's bike which worried me a lot, but it seems all right.

I did want you so all today, baby. Georgie, come home to me. Goodnight and God bless you.

3rd August   Thursday   10.40 pm

I went to town on the 7.20 am and back on the 2.50 this afternoon. Saw Don at the office. He was quite reasonable about it and has promised that he will not say anything to the family. He had imagined all sorts of things and had come to the conclusion that Day must be pregnant! So he was perhaps relieved and that was why he was fairly decent about it.

Sally has just shouted from the caravan where they have been sleeping that she is wheezy, coughing and has a pain in her back, so I have brought her into the house. It sounds like asthma to me, or pleurisy. Oh dear. Goodnight, my dearest, God bless you. Will write more tomorrow night.

4th August   Friday   10.15 pm

Such a fright young Sal gave me. I slept in the same

room as her last night and her breathing gradually got better and at about five this morning it sounded quite natural. The palliasse she had been sleeping on in the caravan was made of wheat shucks or something, so knowing her funny 'snishoos' I think that must have had something to do with it.

Just as I had got Sal settled in bed someone came to the door for the warden (Peter). They had got their house all hotted up, they were Londoners who did not understand the old fireplaces. So he had to go out. Then I had a haemorrage in the middle of the night, so we all had a jolly time. My darling, please come back to me soon, I begin to think you never will. When I look back on the past year everything seems to lead up to this. First I give up business to be with you. Then Uncle dies and leaves me a little money and everything seems to have been rounded off. But I still hope that all this does not mean anything. You always say give you a year and I hope and pray that you had some intuition that you might have to lie low for some time.

As far as the war situation is concerned the flying bombs are worse than ever and Churchill seems to think we shall have rockets any minute now. Lancs and Halifaxes are bombing in daylight. The Americans went to Friedrichschafen for the first time since you went I think, darling. In Normandy we have taken 100,000 prisoners since D Day and are very nearly in St. Nazaire. The Russians are nearly in Warsaw. The King is back from Italy where he has spent eight days with the troops, who are still around Florence. Hitler has set up a court to try the General and officers who tried to bump him off.

I have spent a quiet day as I did not feel too good. Day went to Andover to shop.

Tomorrow they take the tackle to the first farm and start on Tuesday. Whoopee. Goodnight sweetheart, my only beloved. God bless and keep you.

5th August   Saturday   10.55 pm

I went into Andover early this morning, then took a bus back to the Duck and the kids cycled over to meet me, bringing my bike. This afternoon I did a heap of washing. Day went to a film, and Sally made a sponge cake. A quiet domestic day! We played rummy with Toppy this evening and Peter went out for a drink.

I have been very miserable and unhappy all day, my beloved. Having no job and not much to think about I keep thinking that you won't come back and I am going to be alone all the rest of my life. Oh Georgie, my beloved, what am I going to do?

God bless and keep you darling. You *must must must* come back to me.

6th August   Sunday   10.30 pm

I made a fool of myself and cried in front of the children tonight. They had been up to Harcourt School to bathe with the Granville children and I couldn't help thinking how you would have enjoyed being with them, my darling.

I cycled over to the Duck this morning. There was

a crowd of people from the Club there including that pompous man Curtis who says he is doing something important for the Air Ministry which means that the war with Germany will be over in a month. Let's hope he is right. Hal Lawson said not before March.

Toppy and Peter are blinding and cursing because Combines are doing more and more of their work. I really think if they want to keep in the threshing business they will have to move with the times and get one. They have been out all the evening snooping round the farms to see how much of their work the combine has already done. I am going to drive their car tomorrow when they move the tackle to their first job. That should be really funny.

I feel so desperately unhappy. I hate being here. Perhaps it will be better when they are working all day.

Goodnight beloved, God keep you safe.

7th August   Bank Holiday Monday   10.30 pm

Went to the Duck to do my ironing this morning. Kids went to Harcourt to bathe with the Granville children and picked me up at 12.30.

This afternoon Day went to Quarley Fête and Sal and I went to Amport Fête for a couple of hours. I did not think it would be such fun at Quarley and Sal thought it too far to cycle. It has been a simply brilliant day.

At six I drove the Vauxhall (Peter's) up to Wallop behind the tackle and by the time everything was in place we did not get back till nine. Toppy does look a scream in bib and braces! It will be a joy to have them

out of the house all day. I feel more alone down here
darling, than I have done all the time you have been
away from me. Oh, how I wish I had a job. Goodnight
beloved, God bless you.

8th August   Tuesday   10 pm

I've got a little flicker of hope tonight, my baby. Have
just been thinking of one or two people I know who have
heard of their men after 16 weeks. It will be 15 on
Thursday for us, dear heart.

This morning Tops and Peter went off about 6.30
am. The kids and I went to Andover. This afternoon
they went haymaking and I wrote letters, then cooked
dinner for 8.30. Toppy and Peter have gone over to the
pub and I have come to bed. Apparently Peter's new
self feeder which he invented worked wonders. They
got 14 sacks, which is the most their machine has turned
out for ten years! So they have gone off to celebrate.

Tomorrow morning the kids are going to bathe at
Harcourt and in the afternoon the Granville kids are
coming to tea.

Goodnight, my beloved. God keep you safe for me.

9th August   Wednesday   10.20 pm

Much more hopeful tonight, my beloved. Have been
talking to Uncle Colin of all people (he is here until
Sunday, when his two weeks holiday is up) and he
has been telling me of people, bomber crews, who
went missing before you and their people have only just
heard. Oh, darling heart, am I being a fool? I don't

really think so. I feel full of confidence tonight. Please dear God I am justified. I cooked cakes, etc. this morning and this afternoon the Granville children came over. Toppy and Peter threshed 128 sacks today in spite of moving twice so evidently his self feeder is a good thing. Tops is over tired and has gone to bed in a temper with every one. Can't say I blame her. She has a pain in her tummy and it must be very hard work.

Goodnight, beloved. God bless you, wherever you are. Oh, Georgie, please God my hope will be justified. I had lovely dreams of you last night, my beloved.

10th August   Thursday   10.20 pm

Did all the washing this morning then cycled to Chris for a beautiful bath – oh was it good. It has been very very hot weather for nearly two weeks and I think today was the hottest ever.

The kids and I went to see Robin Hood this afternoon. It was very good and beautifully coloured. Came back in time to cook dinner for Toppy and Peter.

Had a lovely letter from Rupert this morning, also one from Shelagh. He is stationed at Chingford and she is living fairly near in a dear little cottage. I think he gets home one night per week. We were lucky being together every night as we have been for the last three years, beloved.

Have just given Sally a tanning for being cheeky. You would have laughed because the shoe I picked up with which to give her the beating was covered in dog's muck or similar dung! I didn't dare drop it but went through the performance without letting her know. Have had to soak my hand!

Did I tell you I had a letter this week from Gray, Son & Cook? Quite a lot of damages. They think all the walls have been dirtied up and that we have pinched wood blocks out of the garage. Shall have to write and tell them a thing or two. We are unlucky with our dilapidations, aren't we!

Goodnight beloved, God guard you and bless you, wherever you are.

11th August   Friday   10.30 pm

A busy domesticated day, darling. We left here at 10.30 on bikes with the ironing for Monxton. From there the kids went to Brocks for eggs and then on to bathe. I caught a bus to Andover did my shopping then back to Mabel's to do the ironing, and home to lunch about two. Toppy and Peter came home soon after having had a row with the farmer for whom they were threshing and walked out. He wanted them to work till eight every night and tonight Peter was stopping at seven because his man is going on Home Guard duty tonight. So they walked out, and will now be at home till Monday when they start somewhere half way to Salisbury, that place where we once went to look at a partridge shoot and decided it wanted too many guns. The kids, Toppy and I have had a good game of rummy tonight and a good laugh. I feel more hopeful again today, darling. There was more news of missing April people in the *Telegraph* today. Goodnight, poppet, God bless you and keep you safe and help you.

12 August   Saturday   11 pm
A quiet day, darling. The kids and I cycled to the Duck, back to lunch and in to Andover to see Buffalo Bill this afternoon. Tonight we have been listening to a radio play called 'Berkeley Square'. Quite good. Apparently there is one on the radio every Saturday night at 9.30.

There was no post today, but I had a letter yesterday from the Winchester Air Raid Damage Help people asking for the cleaners' bill for £47 3s 6d. As they have got it in Kensington with my claim form it is going to be difficult. Have already written for it once but had no reply. I wonder what you are doing and where you are, my baby. I can't believe that you have left me for the rest of my life on this earth. You must come back to me, Georgie. Goodnight and God keep you safe.

13th August   Sunday   10 pm
Nothing much to report tonight, my darling. I have done a lot of letter writing tonight. Toppy and Peter have been out all day so I have had a 'ruin' evening and paid Mullens and Butlers and the car garage. Am going to sell the baby Ford, Georgie. It is silly to be sentimental about it and go on paying garaging. We shall want something a bit better after the war I think. Shall try and get £80.

I wish we had our own cottage and I could have

Margaret, Martin and Robin to stay with me. We could be miserable together. We both feel terribly unhappy when we see other couples happy together.

Goodnight darling heart, God bless you.

14th August   Monday   10.50 pm

This morning we cycled to Grately to the shop near the station where Oak had said there was a pony. We asked Mrs Glover if we could hire it for a week or so and she agreed. Sally has entered it for the Gymkhana. She is a lovely little pony called Jinny but a little bit small for Sal. There is a blacksmith just by the cottage where we had her shod this afternoon. Another pony belonging to Jean Harris (farmer's daughter from Monxton) was being shod and Sal took Jinny into the next field to put her over some jumps bare back. She bolted and threw Sal over the gate! Sal was very brave and was not really hurt. I was worried about her concussion. While we were riding back from Grately with her I pulled up and telephoned through Sally's Gymkhana entrances to Harold and a great army lorry drew up and out hopped John Willie! He was delivering it to Weyhill. He is coming up again next week and going to try and stay the night. We have done nothing but pony pony all day long!

Goodnight, beloved. God bless you.

15th August   Tuesday   10.50 pm

The children were up early trying to catch Jinny. I went into Salisbury and bought Sally a white shirt and

brown tie to wear at the horse show tomorrow. Day is
going to ride the rector's pony in tomorrow as he does
not want his little boy to ride in the traffic. Shall have
to take in a frock for her to change into. Tonight Peter
has hogged the pony's mane, cleaned up her tail and
made her look very smart indeed. She really is very
pretty indeed.

The show starts at 10.30 in the morning so the kids
are starting off very early to get a shady tree to put the
pony under. I shall catch the 10 am bus after I have
cut the sandwiches. We are making rapid strides in
Normandy at last, and today we have made several
landings along the south of France coast. We have
bombed all along there for the last two weeks so it
was to be expected. Doodlebugs still come over London
and the suburbs in their hundreds. The Russians are
fighting in East Prussia and we are gaining on every
front.

Goodnight, my own beloved husband. God bring
you back to me.

16th August   Wednesday   10.50 pm
Oh, darling, the children did so enjoy the horse show
today. It was a blazing hot day and everything was
wonderfully organised. Hundreds of entries and some
really lovely horses and ponies. Sal did not win anything or even look like doing so, but as you can imagine
she was in her element. Day took the rector's son's
pony over for him as he did not want him to ride
through the traffic and as he was in only the first event

the pony spent the rest of the day in the White Hart Stables where Day picked him up again tonight.

You would have loved every minute of it, dearest. Harold Cordy was a bit disappointed he did not do better I think. He got about two seconds and two thirds. I went in on the bus and went back to Monxton with Fred to find out if Mabel is coming to town with me tomorrow. I am going up for a fitting. She is not coming but Gordon is. He starts his film tomorrow, I think.

Toppy and Peter are fed up with work again and have packed up once more.

The war is still all in our favour. Our landings in the south of France are going according to plan, advances in Normandy continue.

Goodnight, my own husband. God guard and bless you.

17th August   Thursday   10.45 pm
Cycled to Monxton this morning to pick up Gordon and the taxi, then went straight to Futofskys. Well of course my fitting was an absolute farce. I had not told them I had lost weight and the suit just hung like a tent!

Carol phoned to say Don has his leave and they are taking the kids on Wednesday. I lunched at Wheelers with Muriel and Stodge and spent the rest of the afternoon trying to get the kids some sandals. Took your watch and Day's and my little RAF brooch to Jays and then to Mr Westley to spend our points. The Doodles were coming over this morning, we had seven alerts before lunch!

Peter took Toppy and me to the Duck for a pint
tonight. A treat to have the Americans gone. Oh,
Georgie boy, come home to me. I want you so dreadfully. Goodnight beloved, may God take care of
you.

18th August   Friday   10.30 pm
My darling, a very quiet day. I have not been out
of the house all day. Toppy and Peter are still at home
so I have been cooking for them. We had a lovely ham
savoury and chippia tonight, you would have loved it,
my own. Day and Toppy went to the pictures this afternoon, Sal went for a ride (they have the pony till Monday) and I had a little nap. Tonight Peter took the kids
shooting; the Withers were finishing their barley. They
brought home a very small leveret. Goodnight baby,
come home soon. God bless you, my husband.

19th August   Saturday   10.55 pm
Another quiet day, my darling. Peter took me into
Andover just before lunch. When I got back it was to
find the pony had a large cut on her rump. It was so
deep I telephoned the vet and he came out and put a
stitch in it. Isn't it bad luck? It would happen just
before she is due to go home. I phoned Mrs Glover,
who owns it, and she was really charming about it, said
it might have happened wherever she was. Peter thinks
someone threw a sharp stone at her. The vet says wire,
but it seems too deep for that. Anyway at the moment
it seems quite clean.

It has rained all day today, the first time for a month, I should say. The war in Normandy is won and we should be in Paris tomorrow. Not much else. Bomber Command are sending out 12 to 15,000 aircraft each day. Goodnight, my beloved. God bless you.

20th August   Sunday   10.10 pm

The pony's behind seems to be going on as well as can be expected! We bathe it twice a day and so far it has not turned septic (touch wood!). I cycled to the Duck this morning. Toppy and Peter got up at 10.30 and went out at 11.45 leaving me to do all the cooking and chores. I'm getting a bit fed up with it. Tomorrow I shall have to get the children's things together as they go away on Wednesday.

You know darling, I am beginning to feel that if you were alive you would have somehow or other got in touch with me by now. God bless you, on our wedding day.

21st August   Monday   10.30 pm

So terribly tired, darling. Have washed and ironed *all* day long with just one break when I jugged the levret Peter had shot with the kids the other evening.

Had a letter from Allen today saying if I want the basement flat in Queen's Gate I must take it now as he has so many people after it, so I have written saying I should like it if it is not too expensive.

Goodnight darling, forgive no more tonight. God bless and keep you, my own.

22nd August   Tuesday   10.45 pm

The children took the pony back today. I am really thankful. It has been a little pest the way it has slipped its halter and got itself torn, though the cut is nice and clean and healing well. I did not tell you Toppy and I had a row last night because I had had Blos to tea on Sunday! They have had a row and are not speaking; so difficult. The kids and I went into Andover this afternoon to get their tickets to Barnstaple and do one or two other odd things. Went over to the Eagle tonight for a couple of beers before dinner, then finished their packing and here I am in bed.

Come home quickly and read what you can of this scrawl, my darling. Goodnight and God bless and keep you.

23rd August   Wednesday   10.20 pm

Such a beastly headache. The kids met Don and Carol at Andover Station and went off to Woody Bay.

I have felt desperately lonely and depressed without them all day. They left about 11 am. I did some shopping, caught a bus to Monxton and then after a couple of beers walked to Abbotts Ann, and had an early dinner.

Goodnight my beloved. God bless you.

24th August   Thursday   11.5 pm   Surbiton   +2s 6d

Here I am back at Surbiton for the weekend, darling. I went to see the basement flat at Queen's Gate and am going to take it, darling. I hope I am doing the right thing. I think I must have somewhere central where I can dump all our things and as far as I can make out the rent is £100. Am phoning Allen tomorrow. There is a hall, small tiled kitchen nicer than our old one, a decent sized lounge about 23 ft by 11 ft 6 ins, bedroom about 19 ft 6 ins by 17 ft with hot and cold basin and two steps up into a dear little tiled bathroom. Having Day at home, I thought I would partition off a piece of the bedroom; on the other hand I could put up a couple of screens, I suppose, to give her some privacy. Mrs McClusky took me round and I saw Miss Harding Finlayson who wants it if I turn it down. If you come back, my darling, it will be a pied-à-terre for us to start out from and I know all the shop people and the tenants in the house. It won't be quite so bad as starting all over again.

I forgot to tell you that Paris fell yesterday, or rather was liberated, so there was much rejoicing by all the froggies. News is good on all fronts, but the Doodles are still very bad here. Windows (cotton ones) are all blown out of our old flat again.

Jean is in an awful flap. She had gone to Stoke Newington when I arrived as her mother's place was in ruins. She is petrified of these blasted bombs and every time the danger signal goes (three blasts on a klaxon) she nearly passes out. It is lovely to be away from Peter and Toppy for a bit and get back to some home comforts. I am going for a fitting tomorrow, nothing was ready yesterday.

142

Daddy and Jean are sleeping in the hall in case of window blast!

Goodnight dearest heart, God bless you.

25th August   Friday   10.35 pm   Surbiton   +*3s*

Allen's secretary phoned me this morning and said the flat *is* £100 and I can take it monthly till after the war. I said I would like a longer lease, I really must have something definite and not be able to be turned out in a month. I want to go where people know you and remember you and also I know the McCluskys and the shops around and it is a good address.

I went to town, called on Lionel this morning and took him some eggs. He was very charming. I lunched at the Maddox as I had an appointment at the bank. I had something from Uncle's trustees which I did not understand. Apparently all the income I get from this £3,000 is £144 per year, 10s in the £ to pay in income tax! Not so hot is it! Still I hope I shall get a job soon. Day is going to be the worry. I don't feel I can have her in town just yet while the Doodles are so bad. What can I do with her?

The grey suit I ordered three months ago, I had a fitting for today and it really looks lovely. I wish you could see me now my hips are slim, darling. Goodnight, my beloved. God bless and keep you.

26th August Saturday 11.10 pm Surbiton   −*1s 6d*

A very quiet day, darling. Jean went to see her mother, so I have done the shopping and been looking after the old man. We went to see some furniture and the rest of the time were at the shop. Tonight Dorrie and Bertie came up and we played solo. While the family were away they devised a better game of solo. The whole thing is more balanced. I cooked a little chicken for Daddy and me tonight and thought of you and Ray when he said he liked the bread sauce. How you two used to tuck into it! When I say I thought of you don't think, darling, that you're not always every minute of the day in my thoughts, because you are my own darling.

Now all the different capitals are being liberated, I do feel news of you should have been through if it is coming. The Rumanians have surrendered and declared war on Germany this week. The Russians have given Bulgaria an ultimatum and we are 108 miles from the German frontier. People really seriously seem to think the war will be over in October. It does not mean very much to me without you, my own. Goodnight and God bless you.

27th August   Sunday   Surbiton   +7s 9d

A very quiet day with Daddy. Jean is still away, but should be back tomorrow.

The Germans tried to shoot De Gaulle at Nôtre Dame yesterday and we heard a recording of it, also a hell of a row in the Place de la Concorde. They were shooting from the Crillon into the crowd, gathered there to watch the De Gaulle procession.

Daddy is coming to town with me tomorrow to see the flat.

Goodnight my beloved, God bless you. Please please try and get home soon, I am losing hope.

28th August Monday 11.45 pm —2d

This morning Dad came with me to see the flat and seems to think I could not do better. Mrs McClusky was out so Daddy got in through the windows! Then we went to the Maddox for lunch. He went off to a sale and I tramped around looking for a brooch with a horse's head on it for us to give Sal for her birthday. I tramped miles and have a promise of one for tomorrow, but it sounds too large. Dickens and Jones have a nice brooch crop for 25s which I think will be more suitable. It is silver or silver looking with a little leather loop at the end. I got 12 candles and holders at Selfridges for the cake. I also phoned up Cecil Cohen who says he can't take an order for six months and can't support anything at the moment but is still keen as soon as the Doodles stop and he gets more labour. I suggested when the kids start school I could probably work at Bow for him for a while and he seemed to think it a good idea. I also let him know I had talked it over with Lionel and that went down big. I shall be so glad to have a job, darling. Vi phoned tonight. Said she had tried to get me for about six weeks but had had no reply from Elmbridge. She was very sweet. But nothing means anything in life any longer, my beloved, without you. I can't think that I can continue my life without you.

I might have to live another 40 years. It could be such heaven together.

Goodnight, and God keep and bless you.

29th August   Tuesday   10.35 pm
Back at Abbotts Ann
Spent all day in town. In Kensington this morning getting a claim form for cost of removing bomb-damaged furniture. Had a beer with Marjorie who was very charming, though again a bit hard on Stodge. Long talk with Vi, Charlie Ingram walked out last week after 29 years there. Bowen objected to him taking two weeks' holiday!

Had lunch at Au Petit Coin with Stodge and Muriel. Then to Futofsky for a fitting. You will love my suit darling, it is absolutely beautiful. Gave Andrews the tailor a hundred cigarettes. Went to Dickens and Jones and got Sally the crop brooch, which is very nice. Caught the train to Andover, taxi to Abbots Ann. They seemed very pleased to see me and were very nice. It was Toppy's birthday yesterday. I bought her a lamp from Daddy (3s 9d!). Uncle Colin sent a message to tell me a pilot he knows wrote home from a German hospital to say he and his crew had all bailed out safely and reading between the lines they have gathered that the rest of the crew have gone underground. He had to give himself up as he was hurt. That happened in April, so I feel tremendously cheered. Poor old darling. I do hope you are not worrying as to whether I am being a good girl. I really am. You can read my doings day

146

by day and tell I have not had a drink *of anything* but beer and have not been out with any other man! God guard and keep you safe, my darling. Goodnight.

30th August   Wednesday   11 pm

To Andover this morning with Tops. It rained in the night so they did not go threshing. I phoned the Bomb Damage Assistance people at Winchester to ask about my £47 13s 6d cleaning bill I want paid and they were quite nice and said it had been held up because the cleaning slips only added up to £41 13s 6d, so I presume it should come through shortly. Have got my face cream in my eyes and can't see much. Ugh! Got a lift to the pub and walked back to Abbotts Ann. Tonight Peter and Toppy took me to see the gipsy, Hedges, who is interested in the car. He wants me to pay him to fetch it though and then is not sure he wants it, so think I shall ask Group Captain Coombes if there is any one who can bring it down to London for me. I hope, my darling, you agree with me selling it, but I don't think there is much doubt that prices will be controlled after the war.

Goodnight my darling, and God bless and keep you.

31st August   Thursday   12.30 am   Surbiton

Letters from the kids and Don this morning. Don is furious with Sally, says she is the most arrogant selfish person he has ever met. Glad he has realised now that she is naughty but sorry everyone's holiday has apparently been spoilt. He asked me to see him in town tonight. As he goes away for four weeks tomorrow I went. I know you will be furious but I am worried about what school Day can go to. We had dinner at the Trocadero and decided that Carol should have Day while the bombs are about and go to a day school wherever Carol is going to stay. She is not staying in London. He is going to write to Miss Nagel about Sal. I don't think it will do her any harm. She has been lovely to me since you have been gone, but is foul to Day and everyone else.

Got back to Surbiton about 10.30 pm to find a registered letter. Wondered what on earth it could be. It was a little white lucky horse, with the compliments of Frederick Miller, Licensed Valuer and Buyer of jewellery!! I can only conclude it must have been one of the people I called on enquiring about a horse brooch for Sal. Let's hope it brings good news of you, beloved. Goodnight, and God bless you.

SEPTEMBER

1st September   Friday   10.15 pm
Abbotts Ann again.

This morning I went to South Kensington to find out the name of the man who examined the flat when it was bombed. I have to know for one of the claim forms. Caught the 12.50 to Andover and met Peter in the town by chance so got a lift home. Had tea out first and met Tops off the Salisbury bus, then over to the Eagle for a beer and so to bed.

Goodnight darling, I adore you more and more. God keep you safe.

2nd September   Saturday   8.15
Lovely surprise this morning. The assistance Board paid the cleaners' bill of £47 13s 6d. When I came to add up the cleaning tickets I find they only come to £41 13s 6d, in spite of the cleaners applying for £47. So it looks as if we have made £6!

Went to Andover this morning to shop, then out to the Duck and back to Abbotts Ann for lunch. A very quiet day. Peter is out, so I am writing this downstairs before I go to bed. Am longing for the kids to come back. Don did not seem to like the idea of paying to let me have Day living with me. So I said if he would pay for her for the first six months of this year I would

151

pay the second six months. I may have got a job cracking by then; I hope so anyway. I wonder if I should
start up on my own, what do you think, darling? If
someone else would put up the capital and I don't have
to risk my own little bit, it might be a good idea. Damn-
able though when you come home and I have to attend
to it instead of my baby, that is the chief thing. Goodnight, my beloved. God bless you and keep you.

3rd September   Sunday   10 pm
   The fifth anniversary of the war, my darling. Toppy
and I went to Abbotts Ann church this morning, not
a very inspiring service. I was afraid I might make a
fool of myself but I was alright. I cycled to the Duck
afterwards and that was not so good. I met Jim Cook
for the first time and he was so nice and asked after you
and I had to tell him. It was the first time it has happened for so long and it upset me terribly, specially as
they were playing Nig's French record and I could
imagine you dancing round the room. Have felt bloody
miserable all day, darling. I promised Wing Commander Weston, the CO at Thruxton I would go over
to the Mess tonight and they could pick me up at the
Duck but I did not feel like going when it came to it.
So have stopped in all the afternoon and evening, crying to myself. Silly of me, darling, but I am so
desperately lonely and miserable without you, my own
darling husband. I don't want to go on living, Georgie.
How can I go on any longer without you? Goodnight, my
own. God bless and keep you safe. I adore you, only you.

4th September   Monday   8.30 pm

Brussels was liberated today and the British and American troops are streaking ahead through Belgium and Holland. France can be considered free again. The war simply cannot last much longer.

I cycled to the pub for lunch and stayed till about 7.30 pm. They were going to open about 8.30 but I felt rotten and decided bed was the best place. Awful fit of depression. I want you so much, my darling. God bless you, and Goodnight.

5th September   Tuesday   9.45 pm

Went mushrooming this morning and picked about seven to eight pounds. There was a letter from Allen's secretary saying I can have the flat for a year or six months after the war with Germany is over, but he will not play longer. I think three years would be better. I think Allen will pay for decorations.

The children come home tomorrow. I shall be so glad. I do hope I shall be able to arrange for Day to live with me.

The Doodles stopped for four days but a few came over from Holland this morning. Peter and Toppy have done no work for two weeks. The weather has not been too good but they have made a good excuse of it. Nippy, their dog has just come in after having rolled on a dead cat or something, the whole house simply reeks.

I wonder if you are hidden in the country somewhere, my darling. I do hope you are not hungry, and now the weather is breaking, cold. Oh God I must not let my thoughts run on. I imagine you ill and dying without me and it nearly kills me. Goodnight, beloved. God bless and keep you.

6th September   Wednesday   10.10 pm

Went into Andover to meet the kids back from Woody Bay. They seemed quite glad to be back. Sal does not look at all well. I don't know whether the train journey upset her or whether it's chest trouble. She had that wheezy business again, also earache while she was away. I think she should go and see Scott Brown again. They both go to the dentist in the morning. Am taking them to Oakley who made such a good job of my little brother's teeth!

Advances and good news from all parts. Russia declared war on Bulgaria yesterday. Now they are begging for an armistice and say the Huns have turned against them. No Doodles again today. I wrote to Osborne (Allen's man), and asked what decorating they were prepared to do. Am looking forward to getting away from Abbotts Ann, I have been here doing nothing but chores too long. Toppy and Peter went to work for the first time for about two weeks today.

Goodnight darling, and God bless you. I love you so dreadfully.

7th September   Thursday   9.55 pm

My darling, a letter came from the Air Ministry this morning saying they did not think there could be much hope of your being alive. I was terribly upset although it is what I have been thinking for a month now, but it seems so much more definite written down. I had my first drink today, about five whiskies at the Duck by myself with only Mabel there, darling. I felt so desperate. The kids came with me but went into Auntie May. I took them to the dentist. Day has to have three stoppings but Sally only one, in spite of not cleaning her teeth. He says he dare not put a band on her teeth while she is at Liss, as it has to be adjusted every so often, anyway it will not be too late by Christmas. Toppy and Peter did not go to work today and now they are arguing like blazes while he holds some silk for her to wind. I wish you were here my baby, and I could talk to you, poppet. Goodnight beloved, and God bless you.

8th September   Friday   10.55 pm
    In to Andover this morning, the kids to the dentist again. Fred took us to coffee while Mabel had her hair done. Day went to the cinema this afternoon while Sal and I did the washing. Blackout is to be lifted on September 16th. The Home Guard is disbanded now and altogether the war is nearly over, my baby. Goodnight and God bless my own darling.

9th September   Saturday   11 pm
    I gave Sally the crop brooch from us both, darling. Harold made her a really lovely iced cake. This morning we caught the 10 o'clock bus into Andover and the

kids went to another gymkhana. They stayed there till six tonight. John Willie called this afternoon with a lovely blonde driver! But did not stay till the kids returned. Neither Carol or Don wrote to Sal today, poor lamb.

We listened to a play on the radio tonight and they have just gone to bed. That man Wing Commander Cheshire who wrote the articles in the *Sunday Graphic* got the VC yesterday. Remember laughing at the Witley being shot down in flames in the illustrations?

Goodnight my beloved husband, I am only yours for ever. God bless you.

10th September   Sunday   11 pm

So cold this morning, there was ice on the ducks' water. The children have been so good all day in spite of staying up till nearly 11 last night. We went to the Duck this morning. Gordon is still in town. He and Bill were down for the weekend, otherwise a very few people were there. I had a lovely sleep after lunch and thought of you. It was one of those satisfying sleepymaking lunches – you would have enjoyed it.

Tonight we played cards after the kids had sunk a large crock in the middle of the duck pond for them to swim in. There are three about nine weeks' old which have never been in water before, but they all swam at once and loved it. There are 11 ducks in the other pen, all about three weeks old. I have bought two of them for Christmas. Goodnight my beloved, God bless and keep you.

11th September   Monday   10.50 pm

Went to see 'In Our Time' this afternoon. Tomorrow Sally goes to Southampton to stay with Chris till Friday. Day and I are going to spend the day there and do a bit of shopping if possible. Had a letter from Margaret Martin today. Poor girl, she feels as I do about the letter from the Air Ministry.

God bless and keep you, darling. Goodnight.

12th September   Tuesday 9.30 pm

We three went to Southampton this morning. An awful journey. The train was 40 minutes late at Andover and we had to wait 35 minutes at Romsey.

Met Chris and her Grandpa at Southampton Station, left Sal with them and Day and I shopped or rather tried to buy some shoes for Sally. Absolutely impossible, so went to the cinema and caught the 4.40 back again.

Had a pint at the Eagle and here I am in bed. Letter from Kate today saying she wanted to put a bit in the Manchester papers about your being missing. I shall ask her to hold off another month, I think.

Goodnight my husband, God bless you, dearest.

13th September   Tuesday   10.55

This morning I had the transfer forms from the Midland re Uncle. Signed them and returned them. This afternoon Day and I went mushrooming and then on to Chris for tea and a bath and did not leave until 8.30! Home to dinner which I had prepared and Toppy just

had to cook. Chris seems better, not nearly so wobbly.
It is inflamation of the spine apparently and the Dr says
it will still take another six months poor girl. Am catching the 7.18 train in the morning to London. I think
it a good thing to see Carol and also Mr Cohen. Am
definitely wondering whether I will start on my own.
Must try and go to sleep, dear heart. Goodnight
Georgie boy, God bless you, darling.

14th September   Thursday   9.40 pm

Such a busy day darling. Went straight to see
C. Cohen, the coat manufacturer. He was a charming
little man but could not start in the West End just yet.
Will keep in touch with me and let me know when he
is ready. Went to Selfridges to the Scholastic department to ask about day schools. They suggested St Paul's
or a convent. Then on to Shuter Fashions to tell Carol
about the schools. She was not back from lunch so went
on to see Lionel and told him I thought I would like
to start on my own, did he know anyone in the Board
of Trade. He is meeting someone next Wednesday and
is making all inquires for me, bless him, then went along
to Mr Kelsall for some money.

Caught the five o'clock train back with Muriel and
Fred. I met them for lunch at Verrey's. Fred had a row
with the head waiter for letting some Americans take
a table in front of us, so we swept out and went to
Symonds' as usual! So tired have come to bed without
any supper.

Goodnight darling, and God bless you.

15th September Friday 10.30 pm

Had to catch the 8.13 bus to Andover this morning
in order to catch the 9.55 bus to Winchester, where I
put in another bomb claim to the Customs and Excise
people. Day came with me and we had to waste a lot
of time till we could get a bus back to Andover. It
rained, to make matters worse. Sal came back from
Southampton and we picked her up after lunch. I am
getting enthusiastic at the idea of starting a business on
my own, darling. I want a big worry other than *you*,
it may help to take my mind off things for a bit. You
can't be a prisoner now darling, you must either have
been killed or be in hiding. Pray God it is the latter
and you will be back with me again one day soon. Oh
God, it is too much to hope for, but I pray for it every
day of my life. Goodnight, my own darling. God keep
you.

16th September Saturday 11 pm

Very quiet day, darling. Day went into Andover
this morning, Sal and I cycled to the mushroom field,
but found the farmer threshing next door, so moved on
to the Duck. Stayed there till two, when Day joined
us.

Had a letter from Bargie this morning. Poor old thing
sat in Kensington gardens all on her own on Uncle's
birthday. I wonder what I shall do at Christmas and
the New Year and Armistice night and all the other
nights without you, my beloved. I can't face them,
Georgie, what shall I do? . . . . . slight interlude while

I go and find out what is the matter with Sally. Screaming her head off because she wanted a drink and was afraid to get it in the dark and Day would not go for her. Selfish little pig, waking the whole village. Time she went back to school.

Goodnight dearest, God bless you and guard you always, every minute.

17th September   Sunday   10.5 pm

Have practically decided to take Peter's caravan darling, at 7s 6d per week so that we can have somewhere in the country to come to for the kids' holidays. It has four bunks, all movable, so that I can put a divan in there. It stands in Bill Glenington's field, not far from Chris. The chef from the Star and Garter has lived there for some years. It is a bit cramped but beggars can't be choosers, can they, my beloved.

Went to the Duck this morning and all the afternoon Toppy and Peter and the kids and I have been moving the furniture around in the barn so that I have got the stuff that I want left behind in one place and the stuff for Queen's Gate in another, and then there will be no bother. The beds, etc. have got most terribly damp so it is just as well the things are being moved out I think. Rummy tonight and so to bed.

Goodnight my own; God bring you home safely.

18th September   Monday   9.30 pm

Took Day into the dentist this morning, then went to the station to arrange for the luggage to be collected in advance. Spent the afternoon making chutney from Toppy's green tomatoes. The kids have been very naughty quarrelling between themselves all day, they are rowing away like blazes at the moment. Have just offered Toppy 30s for her washstand and basin to go in the caravan. Peter is going to paint it cream right through and I don't think it will be too bad. Am longing to get back to town and get going at a job.

The war still goes well. We are across the Siegfried line in many places and as much as 12 miles into Germany in some. There were big airborne landings in Holland yesterday which seem to have been successful. Flying bombs come now pick-a-back, brought by Heinkels. Goodnight beloved, God keep you.

19th September   Tuesday   10.45 pm

Over to the barn this morning to do a little more sorting out. Then the kids and I went to Duck, and found Mabs on her own without her teeth. Freddie had taken them into Andover to be mended! This afternoon we went to the pictures and tonight over to the Eagle for a quickie. Sent Day's and my baggage off to Surbiton in advance, as we are going there on Tuesday.

Peter has been awfully good about the caravan and suggested I pay Flemington the ground rent of 3s per week, he lets me have it for six months for nothing if I pay half the painting cost, and then I pay him 5s per week after six months. Fair enough I think, don't you?

Goodnight my own darling man, God bless you.

20th September   Wednesday   12.5 am

Oh, my darling, it could have been fun if only you had been with me tonight. John Smallwood was home on his first leave for ages and Toppy and Peter and I went over to the Duck about nine, had a few drinks there and then they thought I should go the Eagle and say goodbye to them there, so off we went. Got there just before ten and stayed till a few minutes ago, me drinking beer all the time as always darling, but I must admit it had a slight (very slight), effect, tonight!

This morning I went to Andover and got Sal's trunk, my shoes and paid Harold for the birthday cake. This afternoon the kids and I washed our hair, packed and made some cakes. Then tomorrow we all go to Surbiton.

Goodnight, my beloved husband. Please God bring you back to me. May He bless and keep you safe in the meantime.

21st September   Thursday   9.35   Surbiton   −5d

Here we are all three in our bedroom at Surbiton, the kids in our double and me in the single. We had quite a good journey up to town. Broke it at Surbiton to drop some luggage, two chickens and six dozen eggs! The kids went to the Trocadero with Don and I went to meet Mr Woolmer at Queen's Gate, but he did not turn up. Had a long talk to the Harding Finlaysons and coffee with them. They are very charming and will be good neighbours. They think we shall get glass in there in a few days. I have bought two Victorian square beaded footstools at a new antique shop in South

Kensington, and a paste brooch. Am delighted with them. There was a letter from Hugh when I arrived. He has been in hospital for three weeks with un-diagnosed tummy trouble, so has not seen Roger yet.

Goodnight, my darling. God bless you and keep you.

22nd September   Friday   10.40 pm   +*3s 4d*

Up to London to take Sally to Dr Freeman, the snis-hoo man. He took bloodtests and swab from her throat so hope he will be able to help her with her snishoos. Dropped her at Don and Carol's and was just going to get on with my shopping when I ran into Jack Pullen! So off we went to the Maddox to have a beer or so which we did till it was time for me to go and see Lionel. Lionel was over in Wells Street but spoke to him on the phone and he says the Board of Trade man says it is possible for me to start on my own and will have all the details by Thursday. I am so delighted. I shall have to buy a derelict company. Property in London at the moment is absolute hell and one has to pay the most ghastly prices. I should like to get something in Cavendish or Hanover Square but don't think there is much hope. Tomorrow I must try and find a school for Day. I do wonder whether this pyschoanalyst business is the right thing to do for her.

Goodnight, my beloved, God bless you.

23rd September   Saturday   10.35 pm   +*1s 7½d*

Daddy took the car to town today so I went up with him and we went to Trevor Place to see a Knoll settee which Gordon wants to sell. It is quite nice with a beige cover which is really lovely I think. I don't know whether it is quite as nice as some I know but if he does not want over £30 I think I shall buy it and sell our old one which is so bomb damaged.

Took the kids to Kingston this afternoon to buy school clothes. Sal had to have a navy Wren hat so bought Day a grey one. She looks very nice in it.

Tonight we played solo and so ends another wasted day. Goodnight, my darling husband. God protect you.

24th September   Sunday   11 pm

Absolutely nothing to write about today, my darling. Have been all day getting Sally's clothes together for school. Our airborne troops, who made a big landing in Holland about eight days ago, have had a terrible time but the British Army coming up from the South has just got through to relieve them at Arnhem. We are through the Siegfried line in numerous places and only a few miles from Cologne.

It was in the paper last night that P.C. Pickard and Dickie Campling have definitely bought it. You remember they went missing in February. I wrote to Squadron Leader and Mrs Campling. I remember you said they were a bit awful, but the poor darlings adored you and she gave you eggs. Spoke to Mr Woolmer on the phone today and am meeting him tomorrow at the flat.

Goodnight darling mine, I love you so much. God bless and keep you.

25th September   Monday   9.30 pm

Saw Sal off to school this morning, then met Mr
Woolmer at the flat. He was charming and is going to
give me an estimate right away. Mrs McClusky says
Mr Allen had been there this morning with his sur-
veyor. I am wondering if Woolmer does it up if Allen
will pay. I am longing to get things started and get in.

Goodnight my darling, God bless and keep you.

I am at the end of the book and I thought I should
know about you before I had got halfway through.

26th September   Tuesday   10.30 pm   +*3s 4d*

I seem to have got quite a number of things done
today. Mr Allen wants Woolmer's estimate so it looks
as if he will pay to have the flat done up. I arranged
with Sayers to lay and make the carpets on Thursday
week. Then Day and I went to Ealing and sorted out
the cleaning things, what has to go to Gordon's and
what to London. We brought back the curtains with
us, the lounge ones are seven inches too short! Isn't it
maddening! I am cutting up one curtain to lengthen
them. The bedroom ones are dead right. They are the
ones I had made for Park West and were longer anyway. Am dying to get back to Queen's Gate, to be where
we have had such lovely times together. Had a sweet
letter from Mrs Campling this morning. Judy Lockhart
phoned from Grosvenor House where she was at a party
with an American! She says that Sergeant Johnstone's
mother had a friend who heard the German Radio say
he was a POW. We had a notice from the Air Ministry

saying we were not to listen to those Broadcasts, and
I never have. I couldn't bear to be told you were safe
and then be let down afterwards. Day does not want
to go to St Paul's! So now I must rake round the con-
vents. Do hope she does not get religious mania!

Goodnight, beloved husband, I feel a little scrap of
hope tonight. God bless you.

27th September

My own beloved man, I heard today that Guy and
Johnstone's bodies have been found and that there were
five unidentifiable bodies there which means you my
darling.

God help me.

No. 7 Squadron,
R.A.F. Station,
Oakington,
Cambridge.

3rd May, 1944.

Dear Mrs. Ryle,

I am enclosing a Certificate authorising the Permanent Award of the Path Finder Force Badge to your husband.

If news comes through that he is a Prisoner of War, it is most important that he should not be told of this award in any way, otherwise his best interests would be seriously jeopardised.

Yours sincerely,

T. Capel. N.

Mrs. P.M. Ryle,
9, Hills Avenue,
Cambridge.

ROYAL AIR FORCE

PATH FINDER FORCE

Award of
Path Finder Force Badge

This is to certify that

ACTING SQUADRON LEADER G. RYLE, D.F.C.

79219.

is hereby

Permanently awarded the Path Finder Force Badge

Issued this **1st** day of **MAY** in the year **1944**.

Air Officer Commanding, Path Finder Force.

BUCKINGHAM PALACE

    The Queen and I offer you our
heartfelt sympathy in your great
sorrow.

    We pray that your country's
gratitude for a life so nobly given
in its service may bring you some
measure of consolation.

George R.I.

Mrs. G. Ryle.

18th January 1946.

Madam,

I have the honour to inform you that your attendance
is required at Buckingham Palace at 10.15 o'clock a.m.
(doors open at 9.45 o'clock a.m.) on Tuesday, the 12th
February, 1946, in order that you, as next of kin, may
receive from The King the Decoration of the Distinguished Flying
Cross conferred on your husband, the late Squadron Leader George Ryle,
Royal Air Force Volunteer Reserve.

DRESS   Service Dress, Civil Defence Uniform, Morning Dress
        or dark Lounge Suit.

You may be accompanied by one relation only, who must
be a blood relation of the deceased (children under seven
years of age may not attend) and I shall be glad if you will
complete the enclosed form and return it to me immediately.
Two third class return railway vouchers will be forwarded to
you if you so desire, and I shall be glad if you will give
the details required on the form enclosed.

This letter should be produced on entering the
Palace as no further cards of admission will be issued.

I am, Madam,

Your obedient Servant,

Mrs. P.M. Ryle

Secretary

GVI RI

This scroll commemorates

Squadron Leader G. Ryle, D.F.C.
Royal Air Force

held in honour as one who
served King and Country in
the world war of 1939-1945
and gave his life to save
mankind from tyranny. May
his sacrifice help to bring
the peace and freedom for
which he died.

AIR MINISTRY,

(Casualty Branch),

73-77 OXFORD STREET,

LONDON, W.I.

12th March, 1945.

Madam,

I am commanded by the Air Council to state
that in view of the lapse of time and the absence
of any further news regarding your husband,
Acting Squadron Leader G. Ryle, D.F.C., since the
date on which he was reported missing, they must
regretfully conclude that he has lost his life,
and his death has now been presumed, for official
purposes, to have occurred on the 28th April, 1944.

The Council desire me to express again their
sympathy with you in the anxiety which you have
suffered, and in your bereavement.

I am, Madam,
Your obedient Servant,

J. A. Smith

Mrs. G. Ryle,
58, Queens Gate,
London,
S.W.7.